KIDS
WHO
KILL

KIDS WHO KILL

CONFRONTING OUR CULTURE OF VIOLENCE

Governor Mike Huckabee
with Dr. George Grant

BROADMAN
& HOLMAN
PUBLISHERS

Nashville, Tennessee

0-8054-1794-X

Published by Broadman & Holman Publishers, Nashville, Tennessee

Acquisitions & Development Editor: William D. Watkins

Typesetting: TFDesigns, Mt. Juliet, Tennessee

Cover: Anderson Thomas Design, Nashville, Tennessee

Unless otherwise stated all Scripture citation is from the New King James Version,
© 1979, 1980, 1982, Thomas Nelson Inc., Publishers.

1 2 3 4 5 02 01 00 99 98

❧❧

This book is dedicated to my wife of twenty-four years, Janet,

who has been my faithful partner in every endeavor,

and my three children—

John Mark, David, and Sarah—

who were the three most important reasons I pursued public office.

All of my family has been willing to forego every moment of privacy

and the chance for a "normal" life

so we could help change our state and nation.

Table of Contents

Part 4: Appendixes

A c k n o w l e d g m e n t s

Special thanks to Rex Nelson, director of communications in our office, who helped look over the manuscript and offered his expert "editor's eye." My executive assistant, Dawn Cook, helps me accomplish more in a shorter period of time than could possibly be done otherwise. Her efficiency and energy have given me time to work on the book. Further thanks are in order to Brenda Turner, my chief of staff, whose support and tireless work makes my job not only bearable but pleasurable.

Introduction:
An Avalanche
of Analysis

All our debate is voiceless here, as all our rage, the rage of stone; if hope is hopeless, then fearless fear, and history is thus undone.[1]

—Robert Penn Warren

Just after lunch on March 24, 1998, a sudden burst of gunfire cut through the crowded schoolyard of Westside Middle School in Jonesboro, Arkansas. Four minutes and twenty-seven bullets later, fifteen bodies lay bleeding on the ground. Four little girls and one teacher were killed. A few moments later, authorities apprehended two male suspects. Both boys were students at the school—one was a mere eleven years old, the other only thirteen.

The bucolic calm of Jonesboro—a quiet college town set in the beautiful rolling hills between Memphis and St. Louis—was completely shattered. The unimaginable horror of the crime was only magnified by the startlingly young age of the culprits.

As news of the shootings was broadcast across the nation, the shock and grief of Jonesboro quickly spread across the country and the world. Children killing children!

What could possess children to do such a horrendous thing?

How could such a dire tragedy happen in America's heartland?

Could anything have been done to avert this catastrophe?

Immediately, the painful questions poured forth in a torrent. And almost as quickly, the ready responses came. A myriad of experts and authorities weighed in on the network broadcasts, cable newscasts, talk shows, morning variety programs, newspapers, tabloids, and news magazines. Already reeling under the tremendous weight of sorrow, Jonesboro was suddenly buried beneath an avalanche of analysis.

Although most of these prognosticators and editorialists had never been to Jonesboro, met any of the victims, interrogated the suspects, encountered any of the families involved, or examined any of the evidence in the case, they were quick to offer their opinions, theories, and explanations for the calamity.[2] Invariably, they resorted to the sundry maxims of pop psychology.[3] Most seemed more than happy to seize the opportunity to ride a hobbyhorse or mount a soapbox for one pet issue or another.[4] For some, that issue was gun control. They argued that the tragedy at Jonesboro was "an all too obvious illustration" of why "stronger, tougher, and more restrictive laws" are vital for "the protection and preservation of our free society."[5]

Some raged about the deteriorating soundness, effectiveness, and vitality of the nation's public schools, arguing that "the frustrating decline in standards, the rise in violence on campus, and the lack of safety and security" have made our schools a "literal battleground."[6]

For others, family disintegration was the issue. They argued that "the predominance of single-parent households," "the impermanence of marriages," and "the lack of daytime child supervision" had created "a frightfully insecure environment" for American children.[7] Still others asserted that the central issue was the proliferation of violence in popular youth culture. The seemingly nonstop "gore, brutality, and barbarism" on television, video games, movies, popular music, and the Internet, had, they said, "desensitized kids to deviant behavior.[8] A few even raised the dubious issue of "the stereotypical southern redneck culture." They contended that there was somehow "an intrinsic machismo" in "places like Arkansas" that made such horrors as the schoolyard massacre in Jonesboro "inevitable."[9]

For several days the media's hand-ringing commentary on the shootings seemed to produce as many opinions as there were opinion makers. Each "expert" was quick to offer easy answers, quick retorts, and hasty analyses. But as columnist John Leo astutely observed: "Alas, the modern media are set up for the rapid collection of emphatic guesses on the causes of disturbing news. Yes, it's fair to criticize the popular culture for depicting violence as cool, effective, and emotionally satisfying. But almost automatically, the media now turn tragedies into trends, individual acts into pop symbols of decline. We no longer think it's unusual for far-off commentators to explain the actions of children they have never met, or had not even heard of a week ago. Some of us think this is social commentary. The rest of us think it's blather."[10]

As I have spent time with the grieving people of Jonesboro—meeting with the families of the victims—and consulting law enforcement officials all across the state of Arkansas and the nation, I have become more and more convinced that there are no simple answers to the frightening spectacle of children killing children in our society. There are no quick fixes.

My intention in writing this book is not merely to add one more authoritative voice to the great throng already weighing in on the cause of moral desolateness and senseless violence. Indeed, as a public servant, one of my chief concerns is to avoid the pretense of trying to wrap up this grave cultural dilemma in a nice, neat package. This is no place for bumper-sticker rhetoric or catchy sound bites. I have a responsibility to weigh all the factors that have led us to this juncture, to examine all the evidence, and to sort through all the theories, presumptions, and opinions. This book is an attempt to do just that by sorting through the avalanche of analysis so that we can begin to make sense of what has happened and move forward with hope, confidence, and security.

In part 1, the urgent state of juvenile violence is sketched out in broad terms. We'll explore the notion that at the heart of this looming crisis are the questions of character, virtue, and cultural cohesion.

In part 2, the various contributing factors of America's cultural demoralization are examined. We'll explore how a disregard for the value of life has diminished us all; how the current fascination with antiheroes and gangsters breeds cynicism, disrespect, and selfishness; how trends in youth culture exalt rebellion, chaos, and brutality; how the popular media often exploits and promotes violence; how family breakdown is exacerbated in our society by the very institutions entrusted to prevent it; how both rural and urban poverty contribute to an atmosphere of hopelessness and criminal activity; how America's educational decline often aggravates violent behavior; and how the current national void in leadership, statesmanship, and civic virtue affects our social vitality.

Finally, in part 3, some conclusions are drawn and proposals are made, such as why new legislation is not central to the solution to youth violence. We'll develop the notion that the key to our recovery of cultural balance and social harmony is the vitality of America's basic values: faith, family, work, and community.

In 1838 the great American novelist, historian, and social commentator James Fenimore Cooper introduced his insightful and prophetic book of political analysis, *The American Democrat*, with the following words:

> This little work has been written, in consequence of its author's having had many occasions to observe the manner in which principles that are of the last importance to the happiness of the community, are getting to be confounded in the popular mind. Notions that are impracticable, and which if persevered in, cannot fail to produce disorganization, if not revolution, are widely prevalent, and while many seem disposed to complain, few show a disposition to correct them. In those instances in which efforts are made to resist or to advance the innovation of the times, the actors take the extremes of the disputed points, the one side looking as far behind it, over ground that can never be retrod, as the other looks ahead, in the idle hope of substituting a fancied perfection for the ills of life. . . . It is the intention of this book to make a commencement towards a more just discrimination between truth and prejudice. With what success the task has been accomplished, the honest reader will judge for himself.[11]

I could not hope for anything more for this little volume than that.

Part 1

A DARK CLOUD
DESCENDS

Nothing is more common than for men to make par-
tial and absurd distinctions between vices of equal
enormity, and to observe some of the divine commands
with great scrupulousness, while they violate others,
equally important, without any concern, or the least
apparent consciousness of guilt.[1]
                                    —Samuel Johnson

1

A r m e d   a n d   D a n g e r o u s

Thin lips can make a music; hateful eyes can see;
crooked limbs go dancing to a strange melody; the
surly heart of clowns can crack with ecstasy; rootbound
oaks toss limbs if winds come fervently.[1]

—Donald Davidson

The news is starting to become distressingly familiar to us. Children killing children. The security of our homes, schools, and neighborhoods have been sundered by news of appalling mayhem and senseless tragedy.

On October 2, 1997, a teenager stabbed his mother to death with a kitchen knife and then went to school with a rifle under his trench coat, intent on wreaking havoc. The high school sophomore entered the large student commons area of his school near Jackson, Mississippi. The school buses had just arrived, and classes were about to begin for the day. He espied his former girlfriend in the crowded hallway and walked straight toward her. The two had only recently broken up and the ex-boyfriend was still distraught. Suddenly, the teen leveled his rifle at her and opened fire. The girl collapsed at his feet, killed almost instantly. He then began firing randomly up and down the hallway. Students ran screaming into classrooms and dove for cover. In just moments, the boy had killed another student and wounded six others.

"He was shooting anybody he could find. He shot at me and hit the staircase," said one fifteen-year-old classmate. "I saw fragments going everywhere."

As the dead and wounded lay sprawled across the floor, the sixteen-year-old spoke to his victims. "He apologized, and said he was not shooting anybody in particular," one of the dazed onlookers later told police. "People were laying everywhere bleeding. I didn't hear cries. Everybody looked dead. But he was calm, stepping over bodies like in the movies or something."

Police apprehended the suspect as he drove away from the stunned campus in his dead mother's car. Over the next several days, six of his friends—all allegedly members of a cult-inspired conspiracy—were also arrested. All of the boys were students under the age of eighteen.

A few weeks later, on the Monday morning after Thanksgiving, teens gathered in the hallway of a high school near Paducah, Kentucky, for their regular student-led prayer meeting. Just before the conclusion of their time together, the leader of the meeting—a popular football player and pastor's son—looked up and noticed a shy freshman he had recently tried to befriend, standing nervously at the edge of the circle. The leader bowed his head and asked the Lord for strength to last through the day. Just as the final "amen" was said, the group squeezed hands—and then came the first shot.

The nervous youngster fired randomly into the small crowd— wounding some, killing others. The leader of the prayer group demanded that the young assailant drop his weapon. When the boy ignored him and the shooting continued, the leader lunged at the slight fourteen-year-old, tackling him and throwing him against a wall.

Before he could empty the eleven-round clip in his .22 caliber semiautomatic weapon, three young girls lay dead, another was paralyzed from the waist down, and four other students were wounded. It could have been worse. Police later discovered that the boy had brought a veritable arsenal to school that morning: besides the semiautomatic handgun, he had two shotguns, two rifles, and a small pistol wrapped in a blanket beside him.

Afterward, the boy—hands shaking and voice cracking—looked around at the carnage he had caused and said, "Kill me, please. I can't believe I did that."

The following March, the scene was Jonesboro, Arkansas. A fire alarm was set off in the hallway of Westside Middle School during fifth period, just after lunch. Giddy with excitement, students and teachers emptied out of their classrooms and filed outside in an orderly fashion. On a small ridge about a hundred yards away, two young students dressed in full camouflage

> *Liberty may be endangered by the abuses of liberty as well as the abuses of power.*
> —James Madison

gear crouched behind three feet of sage grass, kudzu vines, and a scattering of sapling oaks and sweetgum trees. As their classmates lined up beside the gym in the schoolyard for what they thought was a fire drill, the two boys opened fire. Despite having to shoot through a chain-link fence, the boys—ages eleven and thirteen—took careful aim through the scopes on their semiautomatic hunting rifles. They were ruthlessly efficient. Shooting methodically and accurately, they scored fifteen hits in less than a minute.

At first, most of the students thought the popping sounds they were hearing from the ridge were part of a prank. "It sounded like firecrackers," said one student. "When people started falling to the ground, I thought it was all made-up," another student later said. When one little girl collapsed against the cinderblock walls of the school building, someone laughed and shouted, "Don't worry. Don't worry. It's all fake." The bleeding student cried out, "No, it's not. I just got shot!"

As the reality of the situation became apparent, panic quickly set in. The children ran for cover. Several students dragged their friends out of the line of fire. At least one was killed when she retraced her steps to help her best friend, who was wounded and unable to move. Two teachers were hit as they tried to shield their students.

The horror lasted less than two minutes. But in that short amount of time, four innocent little girls—two eleven-year-olds and two twelve-year-olds—and one dedicated teacher were slain.

The boys beat a hasty retreat toward a stolen van filled with weapons, food, and survival gear, but they were quickly apprehended by nearby construction workers. That night, apparently unable to comprehend the magnitude of the crime they were accused of, police reported that the youngsters cried for their mothers in their cells.

A month later, the happy sounds of Parker Middle School's eighth-grade graduation dance were silenced when a fourteen-year-old boy shot and killed a teacher and then fired randomly into the startled crowd.

About 240 students from the middle school—located 100 miles north of Pittsburgh, Pennsylvania—were preparing to go home when the shooting began. Police reported that the suspect discharged a handgun outside the dance hall, immediately striking down a teacher—a popular science instructor, coach, student council advisor, and father of three—who had volunteered to chaperone the event. The young assailant then entered the building and fired several more shots. Another teacher was grazed and two students were wounded.

Students scrambled for cover. A dozen piled into a closet. Ignoring their terrified cries, the gun-wielding youngster walked through the room and out a rear exit.

Before the students were able to register what had happened, it was over.

The suspect, who had bragged earlier that he would make certain the evening was "memorable," was apprehended in a field adjacent to the building and held until police arrived on the scene. Later, a spokesman for authorities lamented, "It seems we are now joining a growing list of communities that have had to deal with this type of violence."

The theme of the dance was "I've had the time of my life."

Sadly, these headline-grabbing tragedies are not unique. They are not isolated incidents. They are part of a horrifying trend. Every year nearly fifteen hundred American youngsters under the age of eighteen are arrested for murder or manslaughter. Both the frequency and the brutality of these calamitous offenses increase every year—despite the fact that overall crime rates for juveniles have actually leveled off in some places and slightly declined in others.[2]

While the nation's population has increased only 41 percent since 1960, the number of violent crimes has increased more than 550 percent. As a result, eight out of ten Americans can expect to be the victim of violent crime at least once in their lives. Indeed, the rate of violent crime in the United States is worse than any other industrialized country in the world. Our homicide rate is more than five times that of Europe, and four times that of Canada, Australia, or New Zealand.[3]

Amazingly, minors account for about 17 percent of all reported arrests for violent crimes in this country every year. In fact, the fastest growing segment of the criminal population is our nation's children. During the last decade, the arrest rate for juveniles for murder increased 93 percent, the arrest rate for aggravated assault increased 72 percent, and for forcible rape, 24 percent. Some 20 percent of high school students now carry a firearm, knife, razor, or club on a regular basis. Not surprisingly, since 1986 there has been a 1,740 percent rise in the number of children treated for knife and gunshot wounds.[4]

We desperately need to engage in the architecture of souls.

—William J. Bennett

Violent crime—defined as murder, rape or other type of sexual battery, suicide, physical attack or fight with a weapon, or robbery—has become especially evident in our nation's schools. According to a 1997 survey conducted by the National Center for Education Statistics, many of our taxpayer-supported schools are no longer "safe places of learning."[5] The nationwide survey reported on (1) the incidence of crime and violence that occurred in public schools during the 1996–97 academic year and (2) the kinds of security measures, disciplinary actions, and violence prevention programs that were in place in public schools. The survey's conclusions on the incidence of crime and violence were startling:

- Fifty-seven percent of public elementary and secondary school principals reported that one or more incidents of violence (reported to the police or other law enforcement officials) had occurred in their school during the school year.

- Of the nonviolent crimes reported, about 190,000 were incidents of physical attacks or fights without a weapon, about 116,000 were incidents of theft or larceny, and 98,000 were incidents of vandalism.

- Of the violent crimes reported, about 4,000 were incidents of rape or another type of sexual battery, 7,000 were robberies, and 11,000 were physical attacks or fights in which weapons were used.

- Forty-five percent of elementary schools reported one or more violent incidents compared with 74 percent of middle and 77 percent of high schools.[6]

The findings on disciplinary and security measures were also eye-opening:

- Seventy-eight percent of the schools reported having some type of formal violence-prevention or violence-reduction program or effort.

- Principals were asked whether the school had "zero-tolerance" policies, defined as school or district policy mandating predetermined consequences for various student offenses. The proportion of schools that had such policies ranged from 79 to 94 percent on violence, tobacco, alcohol, drugs, weapons other than firearms, and firearms.

- Two percent of public schools had stringent security, which was defined as a full-time guard and daily or random metal detector checks.

- Eleven percent of schools had instituted moderate security measures such as a full-time guard, or a part-time guard with restricted access to the school, or metal detectors with no guards.

- Eighty-four percent of public schools reported having some level of security—including restricted access to their campus, regular faculty or staff security assignments, and enclosed outdoor activities spaces.[7]

But despite our precautions, the violence continues. Our schools and communities remain battlefields, so our children remain at risk. According to Springbrook High School principal Michael Durso, "No matter where they are, parents want their students to be safe and secure. That might even precede their desire for a quality education." Of course, "with drugs, gangs, and guns on the rise in many of our communities," the threat of violence "weighs heavily on most principals' minds these days." And "anyone who thinks [he is] not vulnerable" is "really naive."[8]

And we may be going from bad to worse. According to William Bennett, John DiIulio, and John Walters, the violence is going to intensify, and the body count is going to escalate. The three authors paint a sobering vision of the future in their best-selling book *Body Count*, arguing that we are experiencing an increase in the number and ferocity of juvenile crimes and a decrease in the average age of offenders. Indeed, they predict that we have only just begun to see the ripple effects of an approaching wave of youthful "super-predators," members of "the youngest, biggest, and baddest generation any society has ever known."[9] This new class of juvenile offenders "could become the most conscienceless, brutal criminals in recent history" because they have grown up "fearing neither the stigma of arrest, nor the pangs of conscience."[10] According to the analysis of Bennett, DiIulio, and Walters, the number of teenagers will increase by nearly one quarter before 2005. This swell of juveniles will have had a much higher incidence of serious drug use, more access to powerful firearms, and fewer moral restraints than any such group in American history. These "social monsters" may actually make us long for the relative quiet and security of the 1990s.[11]

The dire prophecy appears to be only too accurate as accounts of its gradual fulfillment are announced in our newspapers and newscasts.

Just weeks shy of his sixteenth birthday, Craig Price stood before a Rhode Island judge and plead guilty to mass murder. He said that he had broken into two homes the previous summer and murdered four of his neighbors: two adult women and two girls, ages ten and eight. The victims were beaten and stabbed—one woman's body was mutilated with fifty-eight ragged wounds. Joking and mocking in the courtroom, the youngster showed no remorse whatsoever for his grisly crimes.

Described as a teen with a "real mean streak," Timothy Dwaine Brown was expelled from his Texas high school for brandishing a switchblade in a classroom. In the days that followed, the sixteen-year-old's parents severely restricted his privileges—including the right to see or call his girlfriend. One day his younger brother caught him talking to his girlfriend on the phone and threatened to tell their parents. Timothy apparently flew into a rage and beat his eleven-year-old brother to death with a baseball bat. He then shot and killed his grandmother and stepfather with a deer rifle.

John Justice was a seventeen-year-old high school honor student in suburban Buffalo, New York, when he went on a two-hour rampage one afternoon. First he stabbed his mother and brother to death in their respective bedrooms. Then, after cleaning their blood from his skin and clothes, he picked up his father from work, drove him home, and stabbed him to death in the living room. Over the next hour he tried unsuccessfully to slit his wrists with a razor. He then left the house and took off in the family car. In another apparent suicide attempt, he rammed into the back of another vehicle, killing the neighbor who was driving. He later told police that he was angry because his parents refused to help him with his planned college expenses.

When Britt Kellum was nine years old, he settled an argument with his older brother by killing him with a 16-gauge shotgun. Their mother was subsequently charged with neglect, and custody of Britt and his surviving brothers was awarded to their father. Finding Britt too young to be held legally accountable, juvenile authorities in Michigan ordered him to undergo extensive counseling. After four years of psychotherapy, Britt shot and killed his six-year-old brother with a .38 caliber handgun following a family squabble. According to the state's laws, the thirteen-year-old was still too young to be tried in the criminal courts.

Sean Stevenson was just sixteen years old when he shot and killed both of his parents. He then raped and killed his eighteen-year-old sister. Apparently, he had been enraged after an argument with his father over a party he wanted to attend. After the murders, he called his fifteen-year-old girlfriend and asked her to vacation in Mexico with him.

Two twelve-year-old girls were on their way home in a small town in Vermont when they decided to take a shortcut through the woods. They were dragged off their intended path and into the woods by fifteen-year-old Jamie Savage and sixteen-year-old Louis Hamlin. The boys forced the girls to disrobe, then tied them up and tortured, raped, and stabbed them both. One of the girls somehow survived the attack. She testified that the boys bragged that they did it "just to find out what it feels like to kill someone."

It won't matter how many times we pass the flat tax or the sales tax or any other economic reform. We will still go over the brink. Because what we really need to restore is the balance of our judgment and the balance of our moral will. We don't have money problems. We have moral problems.

—Alan Keyes

They said they were just out for a "little fun," but the "thrills" Jimmy Iriel and Robert McIlvain—both just seventeen years old— sought cost a three-year-old his life. "For kicks," the two boys heaved a large boulder off a highway overpass onto the oncoming traffic below. The huge rock struck a car, crushing and killing the child sleeping in the front seat.

Again and again the story is repeated: children killing children.

The trauma of families who have lost loved ones, the distress of communities who have had their sense of security stripped away, and the soul-searching of a nation whose youngest and most vulnerable citizens seem to be more susceptible to tragedy than ever before are not the only costs of this escalating cultural catastrophe.

The cost of lives cannot be measured. Sorrow cannot be quantified. But in addition to the inestimable cost of human misery that youth violence has exacted in this nation, economic costs have multiplied as well—and here is where the economic and social issues of our nation meet. Those who claim there is no correlation between the two need only witness the havoc this alarming trend has wreaked upon our economic bottom line. Fiscal responsibility must necessarily go hand in hand with social responsibility.

According to the Bureau of Justice Statistics, the reported *direct* economic cost to crime victims has totaled nearly $20 billion annually over the last decade—an exorbitant sum, although not entirely reflective of the actual cost absorbed by society since only one in three crimes is ever reported to the authorities.[12] The annual $20 billion merely takes into account property losses and civil court costs. The *indirect* cost of crime—including the price tag for police investigations, criminal prosecution, and imprisonment—adds an additional $60 billion.[13] Imagine what we could do with the additional $80 billion we would have at our disposal if the epidemic of crime were eliminated.

Amazingly, the juvenile justice system is even more expensive to run than the lumbering adult system—and with even worse results, including significantly higher rates of recidivism and lower rates of rehabilitation.

Violent juvenile crime is crippling our nation physically, spiritually, economically, and culturally. The cultural tragedy of armed and dangerous children is hurting us all.

That is why we cannot ignore the storm clouds any longer. We cannot afford to pretend that these problems can be addressed with a few new programs, laws, or curricula. The lives of our children depend upon a clear-headed and even-handed approach to addressing all of the contributing factors to this moral malaise. Indeed, the future of our nation, the prosperity of our economy, and the integrity of our culture depend upon our resolve in the face of these mortal dangers.

G. K. Chesterton once quipped that "America is the only nation in the world that is founded on a creed."[14] Other nations find their identity and cohesion in ethnicity, geography, partisan ideology, or cultural tradition. But America was founded on certain ideas—ideas about freedom, human dignity, and social responsibility. It was this profound peculiarity that most struck Alexis de Tocqueville during his famous visit to this land. He called it "American exceptionalism."[15] The dilemma that faces us is not merely, how can we keep children from killing children? It is, how can we reclaim our American exceptionalism?

How did we lose it anyway?

2

The Demoralization

of America

> *In political as well as natural disorders, the great error*
> *of those who commonly undertake either cure or pres-*
> *ervation is that they rest in second causes, without*
> *extending their search to the remote and original*
> *sources of evil.*[1]
>
> —Samuel Johnson

On the day of the Jonesboro shootings, the Dow Jones average on Wall Street had reached a record high. The unemployment rate had fallen to a record low. Our foreign balance of trade was healthier than at any time in a decade. Prospects for future growth seemed practically limitless.[2]

But as the economic fortunes of thousands of Americans soar to these unprecedented heights, the very fabric of our culture is unraveling: violence and mayhem erupt in our schools; drugs and destruction lay waste whole communities; gangs claim the lives and allegiances of a generation of youngsters; families are torn by malice, abuse, and strife; children kill children.

The Dickensian irony is difficult to escape: these are the best of times; these are the worst of times.

By all accounts we should be emerging from a kind of cultural "golden age." It seems that whatever could go right for us, has. For instance, for nearly two decades, the United States has enjoyed the single longest unbroken peacetime economic expansion in recorded history, increasing our economy by an amount larger than the size of the entire German economy. Inflation dropped from 15 percent to 3 percent, interest rates fell from a high of 21.5 percent to 6 percent, more than twenty million new jobs were created, exports surpassed both Germany and Japan, and our share of worldwide manufacturing output rose for the first time in forty years.[3]

Internationally, the American vision succeeded beyond our wildest dreams. Who could have ever imagined that Poland, Hungary, the Czech Republic, Slovakia, Romania, and Bulgaria would break the shackles of communist tyranny without reprisals from Moscow; that Germany would throw down the Berlin Wall and reunite under a democratic government aligned with the West; that South Africa would move steadfastly toward universal enfranchisement; that the old realms of Croatia, Slovenia, Lithuania, Estonia, and Latvia would emerge phoenixlike from the ashes of totalitarianism; and that the Soviet Union would literally come apart at the seams and then cease to exist altogether? Who could have guessed that the Middle East would be on the verge of an American-brokered peace; that central and eastern Africa would be steadily moving toward prosperity and democracy; and that the long-standing conflict in Northern Ireland would be nearing resolution? Yet within the span of just a few years, these amazing events have come to pass. The Cold War is over. Peace is at hand in the most recalcitrant regions of the globe. And America has emerged as the sole remaining superpower.

In 1941 Henry Luce prophetically announced the "American Century."[4] In 1988 George Bush reiterated that prophecy, and then announced, "The best is yet to come. The American Century has not drawn to a close."[5] In 1993 Bill Clinton boasted, "Indeed, this is our time."[6]

So, if things are so good, why do we think they are so bad?

The answer, according to historian Gertrude Himmelfarb, is simply that "we think they are bad because they really are bad. Indeed, they may be worse than we think." She says that Americans have made the startling discovery that "economic and material gains are no compensation for social and moral ills."[7]

Indeed, in the midst of this comparably prosperous time, a veritable panoply of cultural conflicts now worry us. The integrity of the family is failing in many homes. Educational

> It is impossible to rightly govern without God and the Bible.
>
> —George Washington

standards seem to have utterly collapsed. Crime and violence are, in places, raging out of control. Scandal and corruption have compromised the foundational institutions of faith, politics, and charity. Racial tensions have once again erupted in our inner cities. Abortion, environmentalism, AIDS, pornography, drug abuse, and homosexual activism have fragmented and polarized our communities. The basic values of our nation are persistently called into question as patriotism slowly succumbs to cynicism, bringing public distrust of the government to epidemic levels.

As public policy scholar Os Guinness maintains: "Under the conditions of late twentieth-century modernity, the cultural authority of American beliefs, ideals, and traditions is dissolving. Tradition is softening into a selective nostalgia for the past and transcendent faiths are melting into a suburbanesque sentiment that is vulnerable to the changing fashions of the therapeutic revolution. Thus with the gravitas of their cultural authority collapsing inward like the critical mass of an exploding star, parts of American society are beginning to flare out with the dazzling but empty brilliance of a great culture in a critical phase. The result is a grand loss of confidence and dynamism. As a result of much leveling, even more unraveling, and no little reveling in both, American beliefs, ideals, and traditions are fast becoming a lost continent to many Americans."[8]

Conservative publishing mogul Steve Forbes says we are gripped by an "aching angst," which he defines as the "social equivalent of postpartum blues." Historian Simon Schama believes we are afflicted with "a deep and systemic sickness."[9] According to Henry Kissinger, we are in the midst of a "spiritual void."[10] George Will says we are suffering from "a kind of slow-motion barbarization from within."[11] Himmelfarb argues that a prevailing demoralization has set in because "we have succeeded in demoralizing social policy—divorcing it from any moral criteria, requirements, or even expectations."[12]

James Michaels summarized all of these provocative concerns for *Forbes* magazine: "It isn't the national debt or the unemployment rate or the current financial numbers that bothers the nation's thinkers.

It's not an economic mess that they see. It's a moral mess, a cultural mess. While the media natter about a need for economic change, these serious intellectuals worry about our psyches. Can the human race stand prosperity? Is the American experiment in freedom and equal opportunity morally bankrupt?"[13]

Political scientist James Q. Wilson claims that "what frustrates many Americans . . . is that their hard-earned prosperity was supposed to produce widespread decency."[14] It didn't. As a result, we're mad. And more than a little frightened.

And well we should be. By almost any standard, it appears that our culture is now coming apart at the seams. Despite all our prosperity, pomp, and power, the vaunted American experiment in liberty seems to be disintegrating before our very eyes. According to historian Hilaire Belloc, "It is often so with institutions already undermined: they are at their most splendid external phase when they are ripe for downfall."[15] How true. Although we are at an economic pinnacle, our disappearing virtues are taking their toll, as William Bennett explains: "The condition of our culture is not good. Over the last three decades we have experienced substantial social regression. Today the forces of social decomposition are challenging—and in some instances, over-taking—the forces of social composition. And when decomposition takes hold, it exacts an enormous human cost."[16]

❧

The Human Cost

The cost of our immorality to humanity has manifested itself in various ways, eroding the stability of our cultural foundations. A Pandora's box has been opened and its evils unleashed by the champions of secular modernity, the majority of whom are composed of the popular media, along with various marginalized groups who have found their voice and turned up the volume.

The popular media seem to assert with a single voice that what was once virtue is now vice; what was once vice is now virtue. Violence, infidelity, mayhem, perversity, gore, betrayal, lust, and disrespect have all been sanctified in music, television, movies, and video games as necessary complements of a culture of self-fulfillment, self-absorption, and self-realization.

But it is not just the denizens of popular entertainment who have rushed down the road of demoralization. Indeed, it is now difficult to keep track of the vast array of publicly endorsed and institutionally supported aberrations—from homosexuality and pedophilia to sado-masochism and necrophilia.[17]

As we refuse to stand for morality, we easily fall into serving immorality.

Pornography has become a frighteningly powerful multibillion-dollar-a-year industry in both the U.S. and Canada—with higher sales figures than even McDonald's.[18] It has, in fact, become the fastest growing segment of the American "entertainment" industry.[19] All of the various manifestations of pornography—soft porn, hard porn, child porn, violent porn, live porn, video porn, phone porn, cable porn, Internet porn, e-porn, peep porn, and snuff porn—promote a damaged outlook on sexuality by encouraging an appetite for lust, not love, and consequently invite incursions on the security and liberty of us all.[20]

Prostitution, like pornography, is becoming an increasingly dominant factor in the economic ecology of our nation.[21] With the proliferation of bath houses, massage parlors, escort services, nude bars, and swank bordellos in virtually every locale, the once seedy and shadowy profession has been transformed into a far-flung multimillion-dollar-a-year modern industry—in many places legal, in most others, entirely unregulated.[22]

Unchecked promiscuity runs rampant. The "sexual revolution" has come and gone, leaving in its wake innumerable casualties as all revolutions are wont to do.[23] Recent studies indicate that the residual damage is even worse than what we might expect.[24] Americans are damaged medically: the rate of infection from sexually transmitted diseases—syphilis, herpes, gonorrhea, and AIDS—has reached epidemic proportions.[25] Americans are damaged morally: only 31 percent of American women wait until marriage before engaging in sexual relations, while only 20 percent of men do. Forty-three percent of all teens under the age of seventeen have already initiated sexual activity. Perhaps we should not be surprised that more than half of all marriages in America today fail within the first seven years since they are on shaky ground before they even begin.[26]

Add to this litany of woes the abortion holocaust, the rising approval of euthanasia, and the dramatic increase in drug abuse. The list goes on and on.

How do Americans react when confronted with the ever-increasing tally of our country's immorality? According to Robert Bork, "With each new evidence of deterioration, we lament for a moment, and then become accustomed to it."[27] The cultural bad news that surrounds us is almost too much for us to bear. So we tune it out. We acclimate ourselves to it—almost as a survival technique.

Bork continues his assessment: "So unrelenting is the assault on our sensibilities that many of us grow numb, finding resignation to be the rational, adaptive response to an environment that is increasingly polluted and apparently beyond control."[28]

But try as we might, we cannot entirely ignore the woes all around us because they are . . . well, all around us. Our best efforts to avert our gaze from the evidence of destruction are undone by the realities of our daily experience.

Unfortunately, as the woes increase, the establishments that provide moral support decrease. The institutions that have traditionally provided stability, strength, and solace—our churches, private associations, and community organizations—have been systematically undermined, yanking the rug of moral support out from under us. The values of these ethical institutions have been attacked, their methods challenged, and their reputations distorted.

> *In this actual world, a churchless community, a community where men have abandoned and scoffed at, or ignored their Christian duties, is a community on the rapid down-grade.*
> —Theodore Roosevelt

Attempts to defend and legally promote both healthier values and the institutions that advocate them have often proved powerless. In a politically correct society, many of the evils of our culture fall into the gray and hazy domain of "victimless crimes"— in other words, no one is involved and no one is harmed except "consenting adults." Supposedly these victimless crimes fall beyond the pale of justice. Advocates of this kind of uncentered pluralism maintain—in both their literature and in the innumerable court cases they have undertaken—that judgments on such issues should fall entirely outside the concern of the community or the citizenry.[29] Their argument is that imposing any "community standards" of ethics and decency is "a violation of the spirit of American democracy" and a "contradiction of our most basic constitutional tenets." Any attempt to do so is instantly labeled "intolerance," "bigotry," "zealotry and insensitivity," or "the excesses of religious fundamentalism."[30]

Amazingly, the vast proportion of the modern church has actually accepted this misguided version of "tolerance"—if not in principle, then in practice. All too often, Christians shy away from the biblical imperative to "do justice, love mercy, and walk humbly" in this fallen world (Mic. 6:8). It is almost as if we don't want to get sidetracked by a lot of peripheral issues that might discourage interest in the gospel. We don't want to offend anyone.

"And besides," we carefully reason, "you can't legislate morality in a modern pluralistic society."[31]

⌘

Legislating Morality

On the contrary, as D. James Kennedy has so often asserted, "Morality is the only thing you can legislate."[32] That's what legislation is. It is the codification in law of some particular moral concern, composed and enforced so that the immorality of a few is not inflicted on the many. Legislating morality is the very cornerstone of justice.

Murder is against the law because we recognize that the premeditated killing of another human being is a violation of a very basic and fundamental moral principle—a moral principle that most of us still cherish: the sanctity of human life. Theft is against the law because we recognize that taking someone else's belongings without permission is a breach of another one of our most basic and fundamental ethical standards: the inviolability of private property. The fact is, laws *are* moral or ethical tenants raised up to social enforceability by the civil sphere.

Thus, the question is not, "Should we legislate morality?" Rather, it is, "What moral standard should we use when we legislate?" Will it be the unwavering, unerring prescription for justice of the Judeo-Christian tradition or will it be the ever-changing notions of society?

Robert Goguet, in his authoritative history of the development of American judicial philosophy, argued that the founding fathers of our country recognized the importance of choosing some identifiable, objective standard upon which to build cultural consensus. The precedence they gave to Judeo-Christian morality was a matter of clear-headed practicality: "The more [the founding fathers] meditated on the biblical standards for civil morality, the more they perceived their wisdom and inspiration. Those standards alone have the inestimable advantage never to have undergone any of the revolutions common to all human laws, which have always demanded frequent amendments; sometimes changes; sometimes additions; sometimes the retrenching of superfluities. There has been nothing changed, nothing added, nothing retrenched from biblical morality for above three thousand years."[33]

The founding fathers were heavily influenced by the writings of Thomas Hooker, founder of Hartford, Connecticut, and learned Puritan theologian, who relied on more than popular opinion for the source of law and order in society: "Of law there can be no less acknowledged, than that her seat is in the bosom of God, her voice in the harmony of the world."[34]

John Jay, the first chief justice of the Supreme Court, similarly affirmed the necessity of a standard of virtue for the maintenance of civil stability and order: "No human society has ever been able to maintain both order and freedom, both cohesiveness and liberty apart from the moral precepts of the Christian religion applied and accepted by all the classes. Should our Republic ere forget this fundamental precept of governance, men are certain to shed their responsibilities for licentiousness and this great experiment will then surely be doomed."[35]

Thus, a cavalier attitude toward or denial of any exclusive standard of goodness and morality is perhaps the most distressing trait of modern American culture. In the name of civil liberties, cultural diversity, and political correctness, a radical agenda of willy-nilly moral corruption and ethical degeneration has pressed forward.

Ironically, the brazen disregard for any objective standard of decency and a coinciding defense of perversity has actually threatened our liberties and diversity because it has threatened the foundations that made those things possible in the first place. Radical ideological secularism wants the privileges of America bestowed upon the citizenry as unearned, undeserved, and unwarranted entitlements. The catch is, apart from the grace of God, there simply cannot be any such entitlements in human societies. Great privileges bring with them great responsibilities. Our remarkable freedom was bought with a price—and that price was moral diligence, virtuous sacrifice, and ethical uprightness. The legal commitment of ideological secularism to any and all of the fanatically twisted fringes of American culture—pornographers, gay activists, abortionists, and other professional liberationists—is a pathetically self-defeating crusade that has confused liberty with license.

Gardiner Spring, the eloquent pastor-patriot of the early nineteenth century in New York, persuasively argued that the kind of free society America aspired to be was utterly and completely impossible apart from moral integrity: "Every considerate friend of civil liberty, in order to be consistent with himself, must be the friend of the Bible.

No tyrant has ever effectually conquered and subjugated a people whose liberties and public virtue were founded upon the Word of God. After all, civil liberty is not freedom from restraint. Men may be wisely and benevolently checked, and yet be free. No man has a right to act as he thinks fit, irrespective of the wishes and interests of others. This would be exemption from all law, and from the wholesome influence of social institutions. Heaven itself would not be free, if this were freedom. No created being holds any such liberty as this, by a divine warrant. The spirit of subordination, so far from being inconsistent with liberty, is inseparable from it."[36]

Aleksandr Solzhenitsyn, the brilliant Russian novelist, historian, and Nobel laureate, maintained a similar outlook: "Fifty years ago it would have seemed quite impossible in America that an individual be granted boundless freedom with no purpose but simply for the satisfaction of his whims. The defense of individual rights has reached such extremes as to make society as a whole defenseless. It is time to defend, not so much human rights, as human obligations."[37]

> *Our Constitution was made only for a moral and religious people. It is wholly inadequate to the government of any other.*
>
> —John Adams

According to James Q. Wilson, the shabby ambiguities of ideological secularism are, in fact, a kind of riot of second bests: "Many people have persuaded themselves that no law has any foundation in a widely shared sense of justice; each is the arbitrary enactment of the politically powerful. This is called legal realism, but it strikes me as utterly unrealistic. Many people have persuaded themselves that children will be harmed if they are told right from wrong; instead they should be encouraged to discuss the merits of moral alternatives. This is called values clarification, but I think it a recipe for confusion rather than clarity. Many people have persuaded themselves that it is wrong to judge the customs of another society since there are no standards apart from custom on which such judgments can rest; presumably they would oppose infanticide only if it involved their own child. This is sometimes called tolerance; I think a better name would be barbarism."[38]

Moral absolutes matter. Ethical standards matter. Virtue and vice matter. Right and wrong matter. Good and bad matter. Justice and injustice matter. They matter because the destiny of people and nations hang upon their determination.

❧❧

For the Children's Sake

The effects of a society that—to the detriment of the American family—dismisses right and wrong are staggering: the number of illegitimate births has climbed 400 percent, divorce rates have quadrupled, the incidence of domestic violence has increased 320 percent, the percentage of children either abandoned or left to their own resources has quintupled, and teen suicides have skyrocketed 200 percent.[39] No solid morals means no solid families.

With little or no emphasis on right and wrong, is it any wonder that our children are on the front lines of a social maelstrom? Is it any wonder that they imitate the models of perversity, destructiveness, cruelty, and detachment all around them? Is it any wonder that many of them have begun to believe that violence is a legitimate way to solve their conflicts?

"Actually," says police investigator James Bryant, "it is a wonder that there is not more violence than there presently is. All the criteria are in

35

place for a complete breakdown of inhibition and restraint. The current epidemic of violent juveniles may only be the tip of the iceberg."[40]

Following the Jonesboro tragedy, James Dobson, founder of Focus on the Family, and Gary Bauer, president of the Family Research Council, wrote an eloquent open letter to the American people:

> The sound of gunshots in a small Arkansas town continue to ring like the tolling of a bell: a death knell for four little girls and a dedicated teacher who put herself in mortal danger to shield a fifth child from a hail of bullets, unleashed, God help us, by a thirteen-year-old boy and his eleven-year-old pal. But the bell does not toll only for the innocent dead in Jonesboro. It tolls for us. It sounds for a nation that is turning its back on the moral law it once cherished—a law written on every human heart, yet unknown to many members of the younger generation who have seldom heard it from their elders. Are we surprised at the spectacle of children killing children? Are we shocked to open our newspapers, turn on our TVs, and look into the faces of Opie and Beaver look-alikes charged with five counts of capital murder? Didn't we see it coming? . . . Jonesboro marks a point of crisis, but it's a crisis that has been a long time in making. This small town in Arkansas symbolizes America in a moral free fall, America on a rapidly descending spiral, America without God—an America that has forgotten what her founding fathers meant when they said that only a virtuous people can remain free.[41]

Clearly, the very continuation of the great experiment in liberty launched more than two centuries ago depends upon a sane and sensible reversal of our moral and cultural decline. The great dictum, often attributed to Alexis de Tocqueville, still rings alarmingly true: "I sought for the greatness and genius of America in her commodious harbors and her ample rivers, and it was not there; in her fertile fields and boundless prairies, and it was not there; in her rich mines and her vast world commerce, and it was not there. Not until I went to the churches of America and heard her pulpits aflame with righteousness did I understand the secret of her genius and power. America is great because she is good and if America ever ceases to be good, America will cease to be great."[42]

It certainly would behoove us to heed that prophetic warning—if for no other reason than for the children's sake.

Part 2

❧

STORM WARNINGS

The sin of egotism always takes the form of withdrawal. When personal advantage becomes paramount, the individual passes out of the community.[1]
—Richard Weaver

3

The   Devaluation

of   Life

*The Modern world is full of the old Christian virtues
gone mad. The virtues have gone mad because they
have been isolated from each other and are wandering
alone. Thus some scientists care for truth; but their
truth is pitiless. And thus some humanitarians care
only for pity; but their pity—I am sorry to say—is often
untruthful.*[1]

—G. K. Chesterton

On a frigid November evening, two high school sweethearts
emerged from a Delaware motel room with their newborn baby.
They hastily stuffed the child into a plastic trash bag and threw him
into a dumpster filled with McDonald's wrappers, Coke cans, and

newspapers. When the body was recovered, the state medical examiner's office reported that the couple's infant son had sustained multiple skull fractures caused by blunt trauma and shaking.

The two teens were apprehended shortly thereafter and charged with first-degree murder. Though their testimony differed in the days that followed, both admitted that after the delivery they had simply wanted to get rid of "that thing."

The same week, in the same community, another high school couple visited a local Planned Parenthood abortion clinic. They had waited almost too late. The gestational development of their child was too far along for a simple suction abortion. The counselor advised the couple to have a "partial birth" procedure.

Certain that they were not ready for the responsibility of marriage and family, they did not labor over the decision long. To continue the pregnancy would cause undue hardship—their college plans would be interrupted, their families disrupted, and their carefree senior year shattered. They believed that the fetus was just a "blob of tissue" anyway, so it was best for them to get rid of "that thing."

So they did.

According to Dr. Walter Faulkner, an obstetrics specialist in the community who examined both cases, there was "no substantial medical or physiological difference" between what the first couple had done and what the second had done, though legally "one act was considered murder and the other was merely a choice." The real problem, however, "is not physiological or legal. The debate over the sanctity of life has never been about medicine or law anyway. It has always been about a particular philosophical definition or conception of social morality—about whether or not we can categorize certain classes of people as human beings and others as mere things."

Indeed, Dr. Faulkner implied that it may be more than a little difficult for an American teenager to discern the moral distinction between a legal partial birth abortion—a grisly procedure where an unwanted child is killed during the birthing process by puncturing the base of the infant's skull, suctioning the brains, and crushing the skull while the head remains in the mother—and an illegal disposal of that same unwanted child just moments after delivery. Is it any wonder that such a distinction—where the difference between murder and the right to choose boils down to a mere matter of inches of infant exposed from the mother—tests the credulity of many young people?

Depersonalization:

How Killing Becomes Acceptable

According to many criminal investigators, the first and most important factor in stripping away inhibitions against murder is the mind-set of depersonalizing the victim. A killer needs to psychologically distance himself from his target's humanity. He needs to justify his actions by redefining his prey as a mere "thing."

In his brilliant work *On Killing: The Psychological Cost of Learning to Kill in War and Society*, Lt. Col. Dave Grossman writes, "In World War II, only 15 to 20 percent of combat infantry were willing to fire their rifles; in Korea, about 50 percent were; in Vietnam, the figure rose to over 90 percent." What made the difference? Training. Military strategists discovered ways to condition soldiers to overcome their "powerful, innate human resistance" to killing. They began to inculcate certain psychological mechanisms that would enable soldiers to depersonalize the enemy. Without that kind of conditioning, most men are naturally "contentious objectors" on the battlefield.[2]

According to Grossman, the same dynamic is at work in society at large. Our natural inhibitions against murder are strong. Without careful conditioning, most people are simply incapable of killing another human being. They have a natural psychological resistance to murder. To pull the trigger, lunge with the knife, or swing the bludgeon, they must first systematically desensitize their innate sense of the sanctity of another's life.

In the Western world, chattel slavery was made possible only when people were conditioned to believe that an entire race was somehow subhuman. Abraham Lincoln pressed the same issue when he questioned the institution of slavery on the basis of the sanctity of all human life: "I should like to know if taking this old Declaration of Independence, which declares that all men are equal upon principle, and making exceptions to it, where it will stop. If one man says it does not mean a Negro, why not another say it does not mean some other man?"[3]

Numerous races have been dehumanized for extermination purposes. The Nazis were able to commit the horrors of the Holocaust only when they were conditioned to see an entire religious community as somehow subhuman. Similarly, the great genocidal slaughters committed by the Russian, Chinese, Cambodian, Ugandan, and Serbian Communists were made possible only when partisans were conditioned to see an entire class as subhuman. To acclimate ourselves to killing, we must turn people into things.

Alas, our society has become more and more adept at breaking down natural inhibitions against depersonalization. As if following a military conditioning regimen, we have begun to transform an entire generation into potential killers. Already numbed by the violence-saturated popular media, our children's sensitivity to the value of life has been eroded even more by our legal and institutional contract with killing: abortion.

❧

Depersonalization Works: Abortion and Its Results

Since its decriminalization twenty-five years ago, abortion has grown into a $500-million-a-year industry in the United States and an estimated $10-billion-a-year worldwide. Around the globe, more than 120,000 women each day—almost 50 million per year—resort to abortion, making it the most frequently performed surgical operation. In the United States today, four out of every ten children conceived are aborted, which amounts to approximately 4,000 abortions every day.[4]

Abortion is big business. But what is its cost? We can only tally the lives lost (35 million)—the other effects are almost immeasurable.[5] The medical risks and complications are vastly underreported, so it's hard to be sure of the death/injury toll on mothers who abort.[6] Also, abortion's legal, political, and cultural entrenchment is evident, if immeasurable, at every level and in every segment of our society.[7] Finally, abortion brutally desensitizes everyone involved to the fundamental reality of the sanctity of life.

> *The greatest destroyer of peace is abortion because if a mother can kill her own child, what is left for me to kill you and you to kill me? There is nothing between.*
>
> —Mother Theresa

Momentarily sidestepping the sanctity-of-life issue, what about defining where life begins? The biological facts about children in vitro are not in dispute.[8] They never really have been. It is a matter of scientific fact that from the moment of conception, a child is indisputably a human being in every genetic and biological sense. The miracle of fiber optic photography within the womb has made evident to us all what scientists have long known: a fetus is not a "blob of tissue," a "product of conception," or a "thing."[9] An unborn baby is a child and not a choice.

But we are constantly told otherwise.

Refusing to be confused by the facts, our children have been conditioned to redefine an entire category of people as subhuman. In the media, in sex education literature, in political discourse, and in the arrangements of daily life, we have diminished the humanity of us all by diminishing the humanity of a few.

And why have we been so willing to submit ourselves to this desensitizing process? Certainly it has not been because abortion-on-demand has delivered on its promises. Pro-choice advocates argued that once legalized, (1) the procedure would be made safe, (2) women's health would vastly improve, (3) every child actually born would be a wanted child, and (4) child poverty rates, illegitimacy rates, and the incidence of child abuse would all be reduced.[10] None of these things has occurred. In fact, legalized abortion has had quite the opposite effect. Abortion procedures are still inherently risky—the small print on liability release forms makes this all too evident.[11] As a result of these various medical complications, women in America have seen a massive increase in the cost of medical care. While the average cost of normal health maintenance for men has inflated nearly 12 percent over the last fifteen years, the average cost for women has skyrocketed a full 27 percent.[12] At the same time, child poverty rates, illegitimacy rates, and the incidence of child abuse have all soared.[13]

So why have we been so willing to accept the dehumanizing effects of abortion? Apparently, the answer is simple selfishness, convenience, and base materialism. In the most recent survey of women's reasons for having abortions—conducted by the Alan Guttmacher Institute (the research arm of Planned Parenthood)—nine out of the top ten responses fall into the category of simple personal preference or convenience.[14] As Robert Bork has observed, "It is clear that the overwhelming number of abortions were for birth control unrelated to the health of the fetus or the woman."[15] Lives are taken not to avoid a life-threatening medical emergency, but for convenience.

Obviously, a culture that justifies, defends, and institutionalizes such barbarism is in serious jeopardy of stripping away our natural inhibitions against killing in other spheres. No one is absolutely secure because absoluteness has been thrown out of the constitutional vocabulary. Because the right to life was abrogated for at least some citizens, all the liberties of all the citizens are at risk because arbitrariness, relativism, and randomness have entered the legal equation.

Never will I sit motionless while directly or indirectly apology is made for the murder of the helpless. In securing any kind of peace, the first essential is to guarantee to every man the most elementary of rights: the right to his own life. Murder is not debatable.

—Theodore Roosevelt

To amend this state of moral disarray, there must be an absolute against which no encroachment of prejudice or preference may interfere. There must be a foundation that the winds of change and the waters of circumstance cannot erode. There must be a basis for law that can be depended upon at all times, in all places, and in every situation.

The opening refrain of the Declaration of Independence affirms the necessity of an absolute standard upon which the rule of law must be based: "We hold these truths to be self-evident, that all men are created equal; that they are endowed by their Creator with certain inalienable rights; that among these are life, liberty, and the pursuit of happiness. That, to secure these rights, governments are instituted among men, deriving their just powers from the consent of the governed."[16]

Thomas Jefferson asserted that the "chief purpose of government is to protect life. Abandon that and you have abandoned all."[17]

We have abandoned the protection of life and have passed the unfeeling mind-set on to our children. What can we do to correct this outlook and promote the sanctity of life to our children?

As Alan Keyes has eloquently asserted:

> America has once again arrived at a momentous cross-roads. We are going to have to decide—as we have had to decide so many times in the past—whether we shall only speak of justice and speak of principle, or whether we shall stand and fight for them. We are going to have to decide whether we shall quote the words of the Declaration of Independence with real conviction, or whether we shall take that document and throw it on the ash heap of history as we adopt the message of those who insist that we stand silent in the face of injustice. When it comes to deciding whether we shall stand by the great principle that declares that all human beings are "created equal" and "endowed by their Creator" with the "right to life," it seems to me, there is no choice for silence.[18]

4

A   P a t t e r n

o f   D i s r e s p e c t

*His addiction was to courses vain; his companies
unletter'd, rude, and shallow; his hours fill'd up with
riots, banquets, sports; and never noted in him any
study, any retirement, any sequestration from open
haunts and popularity.*[1]

—William Shakespeare

After ten years of teaching, Margaret Jones, a highly regarded
teacher in the public elementary schools of Southern California, left
the profession to start her family. She and her husband raised three
upstanding youngsters, investing their time and energy in their quiet
suburban community. She volunteered at her children's schools,
served as a den mother for the Scouts, shuttled teams to Little League

games, and taught Sunday school at their local church—hardly a sheltered existence. Eventually, her last child went off to college.

Because of her love for teaching and her commitment to her community, she decided to return to teaching full-time. On her first day back in the classroom, she walked into her homeroom and introduced herself to her students in the way she always had in the past. "Good morning, children. I'm your teacher, Mrs. Jones." To that, her former students had invariably responded, "Good morning, Mrs. Jones."

But the world had changed dramatically in the short time she had been away from teaching. On this day, when she greeted her students, a young ruffian, slouched at his desk, shouted back, "Shut up, b——h!"

Mrs. Jones was, of course, astounded by such brazen behavior. In support of his rudeness, all of the other children in the room roared with laughter. They offered him high fives and hoots of congratulations. On the first day of school, he'd showed the teacher who was boss.

Later, Margaret Jones wondered, "What happened in America between 'Good morning, Mrs. Jones' and 'Shut up, b——h'? And who is going to do something about it?"[2]

❧

An Epidemic of Contempt

Once upon a time, American culture was known for its hospitality, sincerity, and warmth. While always gregarious, ardent, and demonstrative, that enthusiasm invariably seemed to be tempered with a contagious sociability.

Abraham Kuyper, the remarkable Dutch statesman, visited the United States just before he became prime minister of the Netherlands at the turn of the twentieth century. He was struck by the fact that the "average American is by no means hidebound by the formal conventions of European pomp and protocol, which can, after all prove to be rather stuffy at times. Nevertheless, he is affable, cordial, and companionable. His good nature is pleasantly evident and his honest character is genially transparent."[3]

Likewise, John Buchan, the Scottish diplomat and literary lion, visited America in the service of King George just prior to World War II. He observed that the "common courtesy of Americans is everywhere obvious. In the shops and upon the streets, at work and at play, in the midst of their hurly-burly and their hustle-bustle, they are invariably considerate, polite, respectful, and mannerly."[4]

But it appears that those days are all but gone. Observers of the contemporary American scene are often struck by the grating incivility of our conduct. More often than not, we are rude and

> *Without civility, there can be no society.*
> —Samuel Adams

crude to one another, mocking and disrespectful to authority, and irreverent and contemptuous to time-honored convention. We often appear to be hasty and unconcerned about practically anything and everything but our own agendas. We are inclined to laud renegades, rebels, and antiheroes as celebrities, icons, and role models. As the English journalist Thomas Garton remarked:

> The qualities that have made America so attractive, so vibrant, and so dynamic to the rest of the world are the very qualities that seem to be undermined by the current wave of grunge pop culture. The maleficent, brash, and punkish air of the rabble has made its way into the mainstream of American life. Children are hardly ever taught manners these days. There is nary a "Yes, Sir. No, Sir," or

a "Thank you very much" to be found. Even the mild-mannered suburbanite seems to fly into a rage on the interstate when another driver somehow impedes his progress. Race divides acrimoniously. The "suits" are pitted against the "workers." And the everyday conversations of ordinary folks are laced with unnoticed obscenity.[5]

While most of us still make every effort to be upstanding citizens, the effects of this ever-widening culture of impertinence are felt by us all—infiltrating our business affairs, community interactions, and interpersonal relationships.

According to psychologist Marion Ware, we have "grown impatient" with the "basic expressions of tactful social etiquette." That is due in part to "the role pop psychology has played in prodding us to honestly and openly express our normally repressed feelings." The emphasis on recognizing and meeting our own needs has produced an "us-versus-them mentality [that] has crept into almost every segment and arena of American life."[6]

In fact, Ware says, "We now see our world in terms of those in accord with our aims and ambitions, wants and desires, wishes and dreams, and those who are opposed. The culture war imagery is all too apt. But it is a culture war between the imperial self and the whole of the rest of the world. That kind of mentality does not likely make for a settled community. Instead, it is more prone to provoke seemingly senseless violence, dissention, and atrocity."[7]

Ultimately, our behavior feeds a divisive, dehumanizing, and disrespectful social environment—one that may even stoke the flames of disaffection and violence among our children. "Why should a child respect the feelings, the dignity, or even the life of another child," asks Bethel College sociologist Adeline Lang, "if respect has ceased to be an important part of a culture's civil or social vocabulary?" Indeed, she asserts, "By failing to impress on young people the value of politeness, consideration, and courtesy, we are actually inadvertently reinforcing patterns of incivility, animosity, and strife. The pop psychology emphasis of the past two decades or so on self-fulfillment, self-actualization, self-realization, and self-expression has created a barbarous atmosphere where, at least subconsciously, most people are much more concerned about themselves, their interests, and their concerns than they are about those of others. That makes for a volatile situation—especially among the young."[8]

Criminologists have noted that the most brutal juvenile offenders often "have little or no sensitivity to the value of anyone else's thoughts, feelings, or rights. They are self-consumed and self-absorbed." And that attitude is "constantly reinforced by a lack of respect for authority and a topsy-turvy logic that makes it cool to be bad."[9]

☙✗☙

Profanity

Coarse language is no longer taboo. Talk that was barely whispered a generation ago is broadcast at full volume today. Words that could once only be found scrawled in graffiti under bridges and in abandoned buildings are now woven into the vocabulary of our everyday conversations. The pollution of our verbal ecology has become rampant.

Consumer research analyst David Chagall said: "Four-letter words are flying all over the place these days—on the street, at the mall, on television, in movies, in rock and rap music, in five-star hotel lobbies, and not least in the hallways of our schools. In bygone times, dirty words used to come in plain, brown wrappers to be opened only in private if at all. Today, everywhere the public congregates, you are besieged by them."[10]

Was it really so long ago that the nation gasped in disbelief when Clark Gable dared to utter the words, "Frankly, my dear, I don't give a d——n" in *Gone with the Wind*? Were we really such a different culture when the Federal Communications Commission banned George Carlin's "Seven Dirty Words" routine from the airwaves? Apparently so. Thus, says Chagall, "Now on the eve of the twenty-first century, epithets featuring body parts, waste products, and sex acts are so commonplace they seem to be acceptable speech."[11]

Writers for television and film often lace the dialogue of their characters with scatological humor, gross obscenity, and crass disrespect. Parents are mocked cruelly. Authorities are denigrated. Honor is made the butt of vile and vicious jokes.

> *The manners of a gentleman are an outgrowth of his due respect for the life and integrity of others; likewise a breach of courtesy is emblematic not so much of barbarism as of utter and complete self-absorption. A rude man is but a callous egotist.*
>
> —Patrick Henry

Popular music has descended to even more astonishing depths. Abusive and/or pornographic lyrics are not at all uncommon in rap or rock music today. Graphic language detailing the most horrifying cavortings of barbarism is widely heralded as "honest," "liberating," and "refreshing." Anyone daring to express qualms about this vulgar preoccupation with adultery, fornication, and fellatio—to say nothing of rape, incest, and mutilation—is likely to be mocked as a "prude," a "goody-goody," and a "moralistic fundamentalist."[12]

But as distressing as the proliferation of profanity in popular media might be, the widespread acceptance of filthy talk in the workplace, in our communities, in our schools, and in our homes is even worse. Swearing hardly causes a ripple of concern anymore. Indeed, according to Jonathan Lasker in his sobering book *Profanity in America*, many people see cursing as a "relatively risk-free verbal tool" capable of "getting the attention of others, emphasizing a particular point, expressing a strong opinion or emotion, intimidating others, making a joke, or even relieving stress, frustration, or outrage."[13]

Thus, Lasker says, "The most striking trends in the popular use of profanity have been among women, teens, and children. It has been a way for them to strike back at authority or injustice or perceived unfairness. Though rarely effectual, it offers them a feeling of power when access to actual power may be more than a little remote."[14]

Of course, the effect of such a tactic is less innocent than it may initially appear. Indeed, Lasker argues, "Profanity is not only a hallmark of a post-literate society, where ordinary people simply do not have the amplitude of vocabulary capable of expressing a full range of emotions, it is also a hallmark of a frustrated society where ordinary people must give vent to their anger in inarticulate fashion. Historically, mass profanity has always been a harbinger of mass violence."[15]

Road Rage

It is not surprising then, that people who live in a "frustrated society" are apt to lose control of their emotions—even while hurtling down a highway at seventy miles per hour. There are few moral or ethical inhibitions against what would have once been considered immature, foolhardy, and socially repugnant behavior behind the wheel.

In one year, nearly 17,000 Americans were seriously injured in automobile accidents caused by drivers' temper tantrums.[16] Dubbed "road rage" by the popular media, the phenomenon of commuters swearing at one another, exchanging obscene gestures, cutting off each other in the passing lane, tailgating in retribution for some imagined infraction, pulling one another over in an effort to scuffle on the shoulder of the highway, or even brandishing handguns after some traffic discourtesy has become epidemic in many metropolitan areas around the country.

What is surprising is that road rage knows no social bounds. Recorded incidents over the past two years have involved the rich and the poor, the well-educated and the illiterate, the suburbanite and the urban dweller, the young and the old, the employed and the unemployed. "It is almost as if the powder keg of our cultural frustrations is set ablaze when we get behind the wheel of our cars," says journalist Michael Bradbury. "All the tensions we feel in other aspects of our lives explode when some jerk cuts us off in traffic.[17]

"Is it any wonder then, that our children have a difficult time controlling their anger? We have not exactly set an example for them of self-control, temperance, maturity, or even-keeled behavior." Thus, Bradbury says, "Road rage is symptomatic of a culture in trouble, of a people lacking in character, and of a society devoid of the most basic tenants of human respect. It is not a problem in and of itself that can be addressed by conducting drivers' education classes, road sensitivity seminars, or public awareness meetings. Instead, like so many other woes that currently afflict our nation, it is evidence that somehow we have lost our way as a society. And the longer such a malaise goes unchecked the more absurdly detrimental will be the indications."[18]

Social Discourse

Who among us has not wondered at the "absurdly detrimental indications" in political and cultural discourse in America? It seems that we can't really discuss issues anymore. Instead, we argue, insult, and incriminate. Politics is marred by mudslinging. Social commentary is sullied by scandalous gossip, tabloid sensationalism, and squalid controversy.

The rapid and virulent disuniting of America is frightening.

We are more bitterly divided today than at any time since the Civil War. We are divided over what is right and what is wrong.[19] And as a result, "absolute confusion" is now our most apt epithet, according to demographer George Barna.[20]

Instead of the reasoned interchange of statesmanship, hypothesis, and compromise, we are more prone to use what James Davison Hunter calls the "grammar of contemporary hostility." Instead of exchanging facts, insights, and observations, we are likely to merely exchange epithets. Our aim is to marginalize our opponents—portraying them as narrow extremists, misanthropic zealots, or divisive demagogues. We trot out the buzzwords of hate and fear or play the trump cards of race or tyranny.[21]

We have even turned the shouting matches that result from such controversies into prime-time television entertainment. Ratings soar for talk shows that literally turn into physical skirmishes and panel programs that pit adversaries against one another in the most incendiary and acrimonious environment imaginable.

In this highly charged atmosphere, is it any wonder that violence is not only provoked but is actually incited?

Manners

Whatever happened to manners? Since when are the old chivalric virtues no longer viable tenants of social cohesion? We can't seem to conduct ourselves in a proper and noble manner in public or private. Manners seem to be a thing of the past.

> *To establish the fact of decadence is the most pressing duty of our time.*
> —Richard Weaver

Consider an event of the past, such as the sinking of the *Titanic*. One reason for *Titanic's* enduring interest is that her story incorporates all the elements of a classic tragedy, contrasting nobility with banality, chivalry with cowardice, and faith with presumption. It is also true that her demise remains shrouded by numerous mysteries and controversies, making her the object of fascination to trivia-hounds and amateur detectives. None of this, however, fully explains the phenomenon.

According to Phillips, the real reason the *Titanic* continues to fascinate the American psyche is much more profound:

> The fundamental reason for our fascination with the *Titanic* is that she reminds us in no uncertain terms that there is a living God who intervenes in the affairs of men. It is difficult to even speak of the *Titanic* without acknowledging the existence of a supernatural presence at work on that fateful evening. Moreover, the events of April 14, 1912, are the closest thing we have to a modern day Bible story. This is the highly documented, true story of a stupendous catastrophe which can not be dismissed as the

result of random process or mere chance. Everything about *Titanic* was larger-than-life: her conception, her launch, her sins, her heroes, and her judgment. She was a disaster of biblical proportions and implications—not merely because of the size of the vessel or the huge loss of life, but because of the circumstances surrounding the tragedy.[22]

In fact, he says, the doctrine of "women and children first" makes this tragedy stand out in remarkable ways:

> With only a few exceptions, *Titanic's* men willingly gave up their seats on lifeboats for others, thus exemplifying the verse, "Greater love hath no man than he lay down his life for another." The most poignant examples came from the many incidents in which families were split up. Husbands literally looked into the eyes of their wives and children, whispered tender last words, and lowered their families into lifeboats with the full realization that they would never see them again. Thus, one of *Titanic's* greatest ironies is that she became a symbol of duty and faith. Nellie Taft, the First Lady, honored this spirit of sacrifice by mounting a national campaign to raise funds for a monument which would carry the inscription: "To the brave men who gave their lives that women and children might be saved." The structure was built in Washington, D.C., using the one-dollar donations of American housewives. Mrs. Taft explained, "I am grateful to do this in gratitude to the chivalry of American manhood." The suffragettes of 1912 had another opinion. To them the *Titanic* was a symbol of patriarchal

oppression. The philosophy that man should be protec-
tor and defender of womankind was a fundamental
impediment to their cause. Consequently, feminists
argued that the policy "women and children first" (which
led to a death ratio of nine men for every one woman on
the *Titanic)* was little more than a patriarchal sentiment
that hid an agenda of suppression. Leading suffragettes
actually argued that Titanic women were wrong to have
accepted seats on the boats from men.[23]

When asked during the Washington, D.C., Senate *Titanic* hearings
whether the doctrine of "women and children first was the law of the
sea," Second Officer Charles Lightoller responded, "It is the law of
human nature." Of course, there were no formal laws, maritime or
otherwise, which required the implementation of such a policy in
times of danger. Lightoller's comments suggest that he, and others like
him, believed the doctrine of "women and children first" to be a
widely-held and fundamental principle of conduct. Further evidence
that this principle was deeply imbedded in Western thought comes
from an incident that took place more than half a century before the
demise of *Titanic*.

In 1852, the British troopship *Birkenhead* sunk off the coast of
South Africa. She carried the 78th Highlanders, their family, and the
ship's crew. Once it became clear that the boat was going to sink, the
orders were given to remove the women and children first by placing
them into the *Birkenhead's* few lifeboats. Twenty minutes later the
boat sank.

Every one of the Highlanders and sailors aboard the *Birkenhead*
died a grisly death in the shark-infested waters, while their wives and
children helplessly watched from the safety of the lifeboats. In the last

minutes before the boat sank, these brave and self-sacrificing men lined up in military formation. Their band played the national anthem as the ship went down. Like the men of the *Titanic*, the British soldiers understood that in times of crisis, men must give their lives that women and children may live.

Alas, no longer. The debunking suffragettes have won. And thus, we have all lost immeasurably more than we can imagine. As journalist Charles Krauthammer has argued in the pages of *Time* magazine, "this is the real Titanic riddle."[24]

If that "unsinkable" liner were to go down in the North Atlantic today, we could hardly expect the standard of "women and children first" to bring order to the crisis. The great sea disaster would undoubtedly cost even more lives were it to occur in our time—when notions of sacrifice, duty, and chivalry no longer dominate our cultural landscape.

The fact is, we no longer place a premium on civility. Our common cultural currency places much more value on such things as sex appeal, machismo, self-esteem, and raw material acquisition than on courtesy, politeness, and consideration—and that is especially true in American youth culture. Indeed, respectful young people are often denigrated as nerds, dweebs, suck-ups, prudes, and mama's boys. The venerability, honor, and nobility once accorded the chivalrous are now bestowed upon the impetuous.

Perhaps our conception of manners has something to do with this distressing shift in worldview. Often we perceive manners as a way for us to look good—to place us in a better light, to gain brownie points, or to enhance our reputations. In fact, manners are not for us at all. They are for others. Manners are the way we demonstrate respect for those around us. Opening a door for a lady, taking care to follow decorum in social settings, speaking with discretion, and giving due homage to those in authority over us, are not tricks designed to win friends and influence enemies. They are demonstrations of a particular way of looking at the world and those who inhabit it.

For nearly two centuries, it was assumed that courtesy was vital for the maintenance of a free society. In fact, mannerliness was a foundational principle the Founding Fathers counted on in the American people as they sought to construct a good society.

An Exemplary Founding Father

When most of us think of George Washington as a child, we imagine a repentant youngster standing next to a fallen cherry tree with his hatchet in hand. "I cannot tell a lie," remains one of his most famous quotations, and the story of the cherry tree has survived as a testimony to his lifelong integrity.

Historians have told us that this memorable episode in Washington's life never really happened. But it is easy to understand why the tale persists in capturing our imagination. Washington's virtuous life and achievements naturally spawned a mythology to explain their origin.

In fact, we need not resort to far-fetched stories to comprehend how a man like Washington could emerge from the rough-hewn American colonies. He was trained to be a gentleman, expected to live a life of honor, integrity, and chivalry. From the time he was a toddler, he was taught to observe social graces, mind his manners, and respect authority.

One of the most remarkable documents we have from his childhood is a school exercise written sometime in his early teen years. Though his handwriting was still boyish, his grammar awkward, and his spelling imperfect, the manuscript reveals a code of conduct that became his standard of behavior. He applied its principles and precepts throughout his life. As etiquette expert Letitia Baldrige asserted, "The importance of this document cannot be denied; it influenced our first president and therefore an entire nation."[25]

Entitled "Rules of Civility and Decent Behavior in Company and Conversation," the 110 maxims reflect not only young Washington's determination to become a man of significance and purpose, but also the values of the American spirit. Though many today might consider them little more than quaint, they portray a vibrant sociology that we would do well to recall—and perhaps even to recover, for if they were instrumental in the forming of our country in Washington's time, surely their worth is as great today when our country is sorely in need of reforming.

Character is the only secure foundation of the state.
—Calvin Coolidge

Even a severely abridged sampling of the "Rules" makes their common-sense courtesy evident:

- First, every action done in company, ought to be done with some sign of respect to those who are present.
- Sixth, sleep not when others speak; sit not when others stand; speak not when you should hold your peace; walk not when others stop.
- Eighth, at play and at fire, it is good manners to give place to the last comer, and affect not to speak louder than ordinary.
- Fourteenth, turn not your back to others especially in speaking; jog not the table or desk on which another reads or writes; lean not upon any one.
- Seventeenth, be no flatterer, neither play with any that delights not to be played withal.

- Nineteenth, let your gestures be pleasant, but in serious matters somewhat grave.
- Twentieth, the gestures of the body must be suited to the discourse you are upon.
- Twenty-first, reproach none for the infirmities of nature, nor delight to put them that have in mind thereof.
- Twenty-second, shew not yourself glad at the misfortune of another though he were your enemy.
- Twenty-fifth, superfluous compliments and all affectation of ceremony are to be avoided, yet where due they are not to be neglected.
- Thirty-fourth, it is good manners to prefer them to whom we speak before ourselves, especially if they be above us, with whom in no sort we ought to begin.
- Thirty-ninth, in writing or speaking, give to every person his due title according to his degree and the custom of the place.
- Forty-first, undertake not to teach your equal in the art himself professes; it savors of arrogancy.
- Forty-six, take all admonitions thankfully in what time or place soever given but afterwards not being culpable take a time and place convenient to let him know it that gave them.
- Forty-seventh, mock not nor jest at anything of importance; break no jest that are sharp biting, and if you deliver anything witty and pleasant, abstain from laughing thereat yourself.
- Forty-eighth, wherein you reprove another, be unblamable yourself; for example is more prevalent than precepts.
- Forty-ninth, use no reproachful language against anyone, neither curse nor revile.
- Fiftieth, be not hasty to believe flying reports to the disparagement of any.
- Fifty-second, in your apparel be modest and endeavor to accommodate nature rather than to procure admiration; keep

to the fashion of your equals such as are civil and orderly with respect to times and places.

- Fifty-fourth, play not the peacock, looking everywhere about you to see if you be well decked, if your shoes fit well, if your stocking sit neatly, and cloths handsomely.
- Fifty-sixth, associate yourself with men of good quality if you esteem your own reputation; for 'tis better to be alone than in bad company.
- Fifty-eighth, Let your conversation be without malice or envy, for 'tis a sign of a tractable and commendable nature, and in all causes of passion admit reason to govern.
- Fifty-ninth, never express anything unbecoming, nor act against your moral rules before others.
- Sixty-fifth, speak not injurious words, either in jest or earnest; scoff at none although they give occasion.
- Sixty-sixth, be not froward but friendly and courteous; the first to salute, hear, and answer; and be not pensive when it is a time to converse.
- Seventy-third, think before you speak, pronounce not imperfectly, nor bring out your words too hastily, but orderly and distinctly.
- Eighty-second, undertake not what you cannot perform but be careful to keep your promise.
- Eighty-sixth, in disputes, be not so desirous to overcome as not to give liberty to each one to deliver his opinion and submit to the judgment of the major part, especially if they are judges of the dispute.
- Eighty-seventh, let your carriage be such as becomes a man grave, settled, and attentive to that which is spoken. Contradict not at every turn what others say.
- Eighty-eighth, be not tedious in discourse, make not many digressions, nor repeat often the same manner of discourse.

- One hundred-eighth, when you speak of God or His attributes, let it be seriously and with reverence; honor and obey your natural parents although they be poor.
- One hundred-ninth, let your recreations be manful not sinful.
- One hundred-tenth, labor to keep alive in your breast that little spark of celestial fire called conscience.[26]

Even when he was the nation's highest-ranking official, Washington never failed to be respectful to those around him. Like so many of the Founding Fathers, he followed these and the other "Rules of Civility," throughout his life, campaigns, and career. He believed that the kind of inward virtues necessary to forge our civil freedom, would have obvious outward manifestations in a civil society. And thus, for him, manners were no less a component of liberty than constitutions, covenants, and compacts.

Recovering Respect

We yearn for the civility we once took for granted in this great land. We yearn for a culture of respect, virtue, and honor—that which once so clearly defined the American spirit. We yearn for a world in which men take social responsibilities and interpersonal relationships as seriously as George Washington once did. We yearn for a culture in which it would not even cross our minds that children might heartlessly kill other children. We yearn for a land in which teachers could once again greet their classes cheerfully—confident that they would be so greeted in turn.

Such a vision is fully within our competence as a nation—but only if we determine to banish the incivility, profanity, and inhospitality from our lives and restore the belief that society ought to be defined by healthy moral and cultural values.

In essence, we must work hard at the task of humanizing the scale of modern life: restoring such practices as manners, conversation, hospitality, sympathy, family life, romantic love—the social exchanges which reveal and develop sensibility in human affairs.

Although all of these foundational truths are self-evident in the sense that they are written on the fleshly tablet of every man's heart, we must not be so idealistic as to believe that such truths will be universally accepted. In fact, such reasoning will inevitably be a stumbling block to some and mere foolishness to others. All too often men suppress reality in one way, shape, form, or another. But that must not deter us from what we know to be right and good and true. After all, the future of our nation and the lives of our children quite literally depend upon it. Just as they always have—just as they always will.

5

A   M e d i a   P l a y

The incarnation was the ultimate extension of man,
the ultimate technology. The medium is the message.[1]

—Marshall McLuhan

He bragged to all his friends that his kill ratio would break every previous record. Nothing was going to stop him this time. Though he was only fourteen years old, the steely glint of determination in his eyes told them that he really meant what he said.

John Mohavic carefully prepared himself for his murderous mission. He stockpiled ammunition, selecting and arranging his weapons. He checked his sights, his navigational gear, and his bulletproof armor plating. Satisfied with the state of his arsenal, he set out from the old warehouse into a dark, cluttered alley.

He rounded the corner and came out into the street. Snow began to fall. The moist flakes twinkling past New York's neoned hustle and bustle cast a spell of transfixing beauty over the entire cityscape. But he had no eyes for beauty. The dispossessed seldom do.

Around the next corner, the first sight that greeted him was a street fight. A small crowd had gathered to watch two emaciated black youths lunge and slash at each other with cheap gravity-blade knives.

But John moved on, barely glancing at the violent scene before him. He had a job to do, and nothing was going to deter him from that task.

He made his way toward Times Square, then Broadway. It was almost midnight now, and the streets seemed to come alive. A garish kaleidoscope of flashing lights mixed with the wheedling jive of hawkers and the choked cacophony of the dense traffic.

Finally, he arrived at the Port Authority terminal and began to wait for the airport transit bus. Before the bus arrived, however, two security guards, suspicious of the bulk beneath his trench coat, walked toward John. He didn't hesitate. Raising his automatic weapon, he mowed them down with a series of short, sharp blasts.

Pandemonium broke out in the crowded station. Bystanders ran for cover, screaming as the blood pooled beneath the two officers. A boom box was dropped in the center of the waiting area, still blasting raucous rap music.

Almost immediately, several more security guards came running down the long corridor off to John's right. He opened fired again. This time, several spectators were shot along with the officers. A mother traveling with her three small children was caught in the crossfire. She was killed instantly when her temple was struck by a hollow-point round—her brains splattering across the Formica counter behind her.

Quickly reloading, John turned to escape. But now officers charged him from all directions. A fierce firefight broke out. There was nowhere to run.

Inevitably, John was hit. Again and again, bullets tore through his flesh. Yet he continued to fire his weapon madly until the very end. Finally, an armored patrol car swung into position directly in front of him, and he was done for.

Game over. Insert two quarters to play again.

✧

Media World

John was disappointed. "Oh man, can you believe it? I got offed on the first level." His friends just shrugged and laughed, moving on to the next attraction in the video arcade. They had pockets full of quarters and a lot of killing to do themselves before the morning fun came to an end.

John had hardly set a kill-ratio record, but he would reenact that violent scenario again and again until he did. After all, American teens take their prowess at the video console quite seriously. Indeed, one recent survey found that the average teenage boy in this nation spends as much as twenty-eight hours a week killing, maiming, and destroying—as well as punching, shooting, and stabbing; flying, driving, and navigating; climbing, plumbing, and slogging—through their beloved video games.[2]

And when they're not playing gory video games, they're watching murder and mayhem on television, or they're tramping off to see more of the same in the movies, or they're listening to loud, obscene music about destruction, devastation, and despair, or they're surfing the Internet's virtual village of violence, sex, and perversion.

American households with teenage children watch an average of fifty-nine hours of cable and network programming a week. Teens see an average of sixty-seven feature films per year either in theaters or on video—more than one each week. They own an average of forty-two musical compact disks, sixteen game cartridges, and seven computer games. More than 35 percent of all teens have their own television sets; more than 80 percent own radios; almost 76 percent possess cassette or compact disk players; and while only 39 percent own personal computers, more than 68 percent have access to the Internet.[3]

There can be little doubt: electronic mass media have become the dominating means of conveying and purveying modern culture among young people. Is that a good thing? Are we satisfied with the way this revolution in culture has transpired in our lifetimes?

Most of us would answer no in both cases. Indeed, more than 81 percent of all Americans in a recent poll admitted that they were "seriously concerned" or "uncomfortable" with the direction that modern entertainment has taken. Only 2 percent believe that media "should have the greatest influence on children's values." But 67 percent believe that it does—wielding even "greater influence than parents, teachers, coaches, or religious leaders."[4] The pioneering media analyst Marshall McLuhan may not have been very far off the mark when he quipped, "Satan is a great electrical engineer."[5]

According to Neil Postman in his book *Amusing Ourselves to Death*, there are two means by which the spirit of a great culture may be undermined—one, portrayed in George Orwell's horrifying novel of oppression *1984*, the other in Aldous Huxley's equally horrifying novel of debauchery *Brave New World:*

In the first—the Orwellian—culture becomes a prison. In the second—the Huxleyan—culture becomes a burlesque. . . . In America, Orwell's prophecies are of small relevance, but Huxley's are well underway toward being realized. For America is engaged in the world's most ambitious experiment to accommodate itself to the technological distractions made possible by the electric plug. This is an experiment that began slowly and modestly in the mid-nineteenth century and has now, in the latter half of the twentieth, reached a perverse maturity in America's consuming love affair with mass media. As nowhere else in the world, Americans have moved far and fast in bringing to a close the age of the slow-moving printed word, and have granted to the media sovereignty over all their institutions. By ushering in the age of television, America has given the world the clearest available glimpse of the Huxleyan future.[6]

Postman goes on to compare Huxley's and Orwell's opposing visions. As we read what he says, it becomes clear and all too troubling that Huxley's vision is the one coming to fruition:

What Orwell feared were those who would ban books. What Huxley feared was that there would be no reason to ban a book, for there would be no one who wanted to read one. Orwell feared those who would deprive us of information. Huxley feared those who would give us so much that we would be reduced to passivity and egoism. Orwell feared that the truth would be concealed from us. Huxley feared the truth would be drowned in a sea of irrelevance. Orwell feared we would become a captive culture. Huxley feared we would become a trivial culture, preoccupied with some equivalent of the feelies, the orgy porgy, and the centrifugal bumblepuppy. As Huxley remarked in *Brave New World Revisited*, the civil libertarians and rationalists who are ever on the alert to oppose tyranny failed to take into account man's almost infinite appetite for distractions. In *1984*, Huxley added, people are controlled by inflicting pain. In *Brave New World*, they are controlled by inflicting pleasure. In short, Orwell feared that what we hate will ruin us. Huxley feared that what we love will ruin us. We must face the possibility that Huxley, not Orwell, was right.[7]

We can see now that Huxley was right, for we have already begun the process of "amusing ourselves to death."[8]

Television

One considerable source of amusement is television, which has become America's drug of choice—a kind of "electronic valium."[9] Virtually everyone across this vast land is using it.

More than 98 percent of all households have at least one television set. In fact, more American households have televisions than have indoor plumbing. Not surprisingly, American children watch an inordinate amount of programming. Preschoolers watch an average of more than twenty-seven hours each week—more than four hours per day. On school nights, American teens limit their television consumption to only about three hours per night.[10] In contrast though, they spend about fifty-four minutes on homework, less than sixteen minutes reading, about fourteen minutes alone with their mothers, and less than five minutes with their fathers.[11]

And what is it that we are all watching so obsessively?

Certainly, television shows do not portray real life. A survey of one week's prime-time network and major cable channel offerings revealed a wide disparity between the lives of Americans and the world of television:

- Of the seventy-three sex scenes shown that week, thirty-one were of unmarried heterosexual adults, twenty-three were adulterous, four were between married couples, two involved male homosexual couples, five involved lesbian couples, and eight involved unmarried, heterosexual teens.

> *Television enables you to be entertained in your home by people you wouldn't have in your home.*
>
> —David Frost

- Despite the fact that nearly half of all Americans attend church at least once a week, only four characters that week in prime time showed any evidence of religious belief. Only one of them appeared to be an orthodox Christian—and she was an angel.
- More than half of the programs aired that week portrayed at least one violent act. The final count included forty-seven murders, eighty-eight assaults, and twenty-three accidental deaths.
- Graphic violence—meaning that blood, assault, or anguish was clearly portrayed—predominated in prime time that week with more than 209 occurrences.[12]

The average American child watches 8,000 made-for-television murders and 100,000 acts of violence by the end of grade school.[13] By the time the child has graduated from high school, that number will have doubled.[14] The casual carnage is woven into supposedly real-life situations with amazing alacrity. One survey found that situation comedies, cartoons, and family dramas were just as likely to feature violence as police procedurals, medical dramas, and period masques.[15]

While programming has certainly become more explicit, brazen, and perverse in recent years, television has always been a bastion of mindless barbarism. As early as 1961—Newton Minow, at that time the chairman of the Federal Communications Commission—assessed the merits of television in a scathing critique:

> When television is bad, there is nothing worse. I invite you to sit down in front of your television set when your station goes on the air and stay there without a book, magazine, newspaper, profit-and-loss sheet, or rating book to distract you—and keep your eyes glued to that set until the station signs off. I can assure you that you will observe a vast wasteland. You will see a procession of game shows, violence, audience participation shows, formula comedies about totally unbelievable families, blood and thunder, mayhem, violence, sadism, murder, western bad men, western good men, private eyes, gangsters, more violence, and cartoons. And endlessly, commercials—many screaming, cajoling, and offending. And most of all boredom. True you will see a few things you will enjoy. But they will be very, very few. And if you think I exaggerate, try it.[16]

Eight years later, the Milton Eisenhower Commission reported, "We are deeply troubled by the television's constant portrayal of violence in pandering to a public preoccupation with violence that television itself has helped to generate."[17]

In 1992, the National Commission on Children made a plea for a sane program of internal regulation and self-restraint in the television industry: "Pervasive images of crime, violence, and sexuality expose children and youth to situations and problems that often conflict with the common values of our society. Accordingly, we call upon the media, especially television, to discipline themselves so that they are a part of the solution to our society's serious problems rather than a cause."[18]

Alas, the plea fell on deaf ears. With the proliferation of cable channel options has come a proliferation of the very worst elements of broadcast entertainment in a vastly enlarged menu of offerings heretofore unimagined and unimaginable. Consequently, more channels exist to play more mental trash to appeal to more people. The situation has gone from bad to worse.

Movies

Whatever is wrong with television is doubly wrong with Hollywood films. Television's flimsy restraints on profane language, gratuitous gore, and graphic sexuality are altogether absent in the movies. Things have gone so far that renowned film critic Michael Medved has lamented, "I don't think I can review movies much longer. It is an assault on the senses and an assault on the spirit."[19]

According to a recent nationwide poll, 80 percent of Americans believe that there is too much profanity in Hollywood productions. More than 60 percent believe there is too much gratuitous violence. About 55 percent believe that graphic sexuality and scatological subjects detract from the value of a film. And 40 percent believe that they have been "desensitized" to issues of moral concern by their viewing habits.[20]

Nevertheless, we continue to patronize the theaters, pay-per-view channels, and video stores in record numbers. Every year there are more than 4 billion videocassette rentals. Almost 2 billion subscribers watched one particular pay-per-view program. And despite rising ticket prices, and competition from cable and video rentals, box office receipts have risen every year for the past decade.[21]

And in our insatiable appetite for more movie entertainment, Americans are consuming more violence, more perversion, and more sacrilege than ever before. According to director Alan Pakula: "Movie violence is like eating salt. The more you eat, the more you need to eat to taste it at all. People are becoming immune to the effects: death counts have quadrupled, the blast power is increasing by the megaton, and they're becoming deaf to it. They've developed an insatiability for raw sensation."[22]

> *Popular entertainment sells sex, pornography, violence, vulgarity, attacks on traditional forms of authority and outright perversion . . . . The culture has changed, is changing, and the change is for the worse. The worst is the leading edge.*
>
> —Robert Bork

Once upon a time, Hollywood regulated itself according to a self-imposed standard of moral restraint designed to uphold social virtue and cultural cohesion. An industry committee, the Hays Association, checked every film for content expressing "blasphemy, filthy language, explicit eroticism or perversion, superfluous violence or brutality, ethnic slurs, or anti-American sentiment."[23] It made certain that any offensive material was edited out—otherwise, the film was unable to achieve general release to the public.

This cooperative association for self-censorship sought to uphold community values in virtually every arena that the art of film might touch. Thus, according to the Hays Code:

- "The technique of murder must be presented in a way that will not inspire imitation; brutal killings are not to be presented in detail; revenge in modern times shall not be justified.
- Theft, robbery, safe-cracking, and dynamiting of trains, mines, buildings, etc. should not be detailed in method; arson must be subject to the same safeguards; the use of firearms should be restricted to essentials; methods of smuggling should not be presented.
- Illegal drug traffic must never be presented.
- The sanctity of the institution of marriage and the home shall be upheld. Pictures shall not infer that low forms of sex relationship are the accepted or common thing.
- Adultery, sometimes necessary plot material, must not be explicitly treated or justified, or presented attractively.
- Scenes of passion should not be introduced when not essential to the plot. In general, passion should be so treated that these scenes do not stimulate the lower and baser element.
- Seduction or rape should never be more than suggested, and only when essential for the plot, and even then never shown by explicit method; they are never the proper subject for comedy.
- Sex perversion or inference of it is forbidden.
- The treatment of low, disgusting, though not necessarily evil subjects, should be subject to the dictates of good taste and regard for the sensibilities of the audience.
- Obscenity in words, gesture, reference, song, joke, or by suggestion is forbidden.

- Pointed vulgarity or vulgar expressions, however used, are forbidden.
- Complete nudity is never permitted. This includes nudity in fact, or in silhouette, or any lecherous or licentious notice thereof by other characters in the picture.
- No film or episode may throw ridicule on any religious faith.
- Ministers of religion, in their character as such, should not be used as comic characters or as villains."[24]

What sort of movies could possibly have been made under these kinds of restrictions, you ask? Many of Hollywood's classics met these restrictions: *All Quiet on the Western Front, It's a Wonderful Life, Moby Dick, Gone with the Wind, Citizen Kane, Casablanca, The Maltese Falcon,* and *East of Eden.*

During the entire span of Hollywood's "Golden Age," the Hays Code was honored. But no more. It seems that Hollywood filmmakers go out of their way to see how far they can stretch the viewing public. Indeed, one heralded, Oscar-winning screenwriter and director asserted: "I prefer rude, rowdy stuff because that's one of the easiest ways to conquer an audience's disbelief. The more realistic the violence and the steamier the sex, the more likely you will be to forget you are watching a film."[25]

⤫

Music

The great Scottish literary historian Thomas Carlyle once said, "Sing me the songs of a generation and I'll tell you the soul of the times." Alas, we would have a hard time taking Carlyle up on his proposition. The fact is, much of our popular music is simply not singable because of its offensive material. Many rap and rock songs have gone far beyond the mere bounds of pornography to vile brutality, scatological filth, sadistic nihilism, blasphemous irreverence, and provocative decadence.

Pop music has almost always been sentimental, sappy, and insubstantial. In the forties, it tended to be romantic. In the fifties, it was silly. In the sixties, it was psychedelic. In the seventies, it was carnal. In the eighties, it was sensual. But it the nineties, it has become nightmarishly barbaric. With the advent of grunge rock, neo-punk, industrial rock, hip hop, goth rock, death metal, gangsta rap, rage rock, metal frenzy, rave rock, and speed metal, a new wave of wildly angry music—with minimal melody lines or hooks, harsh and distorted electronics, incessant syncopations, and vile lyrics—has swept onto center stage. Steeped in a hopeless worldview of suicide, occultism, sexual abuse, self-mutilation, brutal sadism, defecation, and random revenge, the music is depressing, dark, and deleterious.

During a recent six-week period, the lyrics of the top twenty best-selling alternative rock, hip hop, and rap disks were examined. Researchers listened to every song on each of the disks. They found that 100 percent of the disks feature songs that celebrated illicit sex or drug abuse. Almost 89 percent openly portray suicide as a viable option. About 77 percent mock authority figures. Almost 61 percent profile violent acts, including murder, rape, and molestation. Nearly 42 percent advocate anarchy. And 28 percent denigrated traditional religion. One disk alone had 243 uses of the "f-word," 121 explicit terms for male or female genitalia, 92 allusions to or descriptions of oral sex, 64 graphic descriptions of bodily elimination or discharge, 43 ethnic slurs, 24 allusions to assaulting or killing police officers, and 188 pronouncements of cursing, anathema, or damnation.[26]

According to Michael Bywater: "The music industry has somehow reduced humanity's greatest achievement—a near universal language of pure transcendence—into a knuckle-dragging sub-pidgin of grunts and snarls, capable of fully expressing only the more pointless forms of violence and the more brutal forms of sex."[27]

A steady diet of such music is likely to have a profound effect on anyone—but it especially impacts impressionable adolescents. And teens have more than a steady diet of it: between the seventh and twelfth grades, the average American teen listens to 10,500 hours of rock music, just slightly less than the total number of hours spent in the classroom from kindergarten to graduation.[28]

According to the Council on Scientific Affairs of the American Medical Association: "Over the past decade, the messages portrayed by certain types of rock music [have presented] a real threat to the physical health and well-being of especially vulnerable children and adolescents. Lyrics promoting drug and alcohol abuse, sexual exploitation, bigotry, and racism are combined with rhythms and intensities that appeal to youth. Physicians should know about these potentially destructive themes."[29] Indeed, we should all know about their existence and how to avoid them.

∾⤫∾

Conditioning Process

Add to television, movies, and music the violent or perverse content in many video games and Internet sites, and you have a prescription for cultural disaster. At every turn the vision, the standards, and the precepts that provoked the great flowering of Western civilization are profligately subverted—and that makes for a terribly unstable society. But it also makes for a violent society.

According to juvenile criminologists, there are direct and obvious correlations between deleterious pop culture and youth violence. Indeed, in virtually every case of violent teen crime there is evidence of heavy involvement in—and even deliberate imitation of—depraved lyrics in music, violent films, brutal video games, or decadent television programming.[30]

Essentially, the entertainment industry is conditioning kids to kill. It is training them by wearing down their natural resistance, by inciting their baser passions, and by detailing the methods, procedures, and techniques of destructive behavior. In many ways, the mass media has unknowingly aped the military's training regimen for depersonalization. According to military historian Lt. Col. Dave Grossman: "Men are recruited at a psychologically malleable age. They are distanced from their enemy psychologically, taught to hate, and dehumanize. They are given the threat of authority, the absolution and pressure of groups. Even then they are resistant and have trouble killing. They shoot in the air; they find nonviolent tasks to occupy them. And so they still need to be conditioned. The conditioning is astoundingly effective, but there is a psychological price to pay."[31]

Amazingly, Grossman says, pop culture does follows that same procedure to frightening effect: "Violent movies are targeted at the young, both men and women, the same audience the military has determined to be most susceptible for its killing purposes. Violent video games hardwire young people for shooting at humans. The entertainment industry conditions the young in exactly the same way the military does."[32]

In essence what we have done is brainwash our children to hate our culture, to hate our mores, to hate beauty and significance, to hate authority and substance, to hate us, and to hate each other. And we have effectively trained them to do something about all that hate. So why are we surprised when they do?

Syndicated journalist Charles Krauthammer said it well: "Today's mass culture would not know an idea, subversive or otherwise, if it met one. It traffics instead in sensibility and image, with a premium on the degrading: rap lyrics in which women are for using and abusing, movies in which violence is administered with a smirk and a smile. Casual cruelty, knowing sex. Nothing could be better designed to rob youth of its most ephemeral gift: innocence. The ultimate effect of our mass culture is to make children older than their years, to turn them into the knowing, cynical pseudo-adult that is by now the model kid of the TV sitcom. It is a crime against children to make them older than their years. And it won't do for the purveyors of cynicism to hide behind the First Amendment. Of course they have the right to publish and peddle this trash to kids. But they should have the decency not to."[33]

6

F a m i l i e s   u n d e r   S i e g e

*Any woodsman can tell you that in a broken and sun-
dered nest, one can hardly expect to find more than a
precious few whole eggs. So it is with the family.*[1]

—Thomas Jefferson

Until eight years ago, Kathi Tannenbaum had been a traditional homemaker. She had dedicated herself to building a comfortable life with her husband, Jacob, and her sons, Aaron and Alex. For twenty-two years, she was the epitome of the committed and caring wife, mother, and housekeeper.

But then one day Kathi's son Aaron was killed in a tragic automobile accident. Jacob took to alcohol for consolation. Three months after the accident, Jacob sold the family's small electrical supply business and two weeks after that, he filed for divorce. The judge in divorce court awarded Kathi an equal property settlement and custody of their son, but she was unable to demonstrate that Jacob had any other assets than the three-flat Brooklyn brownstone that had been their home for ten years.

"He had a fantastic lawyer and they were able to shelter the business assets. I didn't get a dime," she lamented, "and since New York has a no-fault divorce law, I wasn't entitled to any alimony. And I only got a pittance for child support."

Suddenly at age forty-three, Kathi Tannenbaum was alone. She had no job. No job history. No job skills. No job leads. No job references. Nothing.

Her share from the sale of the brownstone came to just under $45,000. But after paying her half of the back debts, she was left with a mere $39,000. And with that, she was to start a new life with her son.

Kathi immediately moved into a small apartment with young Alex and went to work as a waitress. She made about $900 a month, including tips. Meanwhile, Jacob had quit drinking, gone back to the electrical supply business, and remarried. His annual income returned to his pre-divorce level—nearly $65,000 a year—and he and his young new wife purchased a home in the Long Island suburbs. Nevertheless, he failed to make more than half of his child support payments.

"I'll admit it right off," Kathi recalled, "I became very bitter at that point. Very bitter. Why he should have been able to just pick up and carry on as if nothing had happened just escaped me. Yes, indeed, I was bitter."

Worried about her, several of Kathi's old friends encouraged her to take up a hobby, go out, do some volunteer work for a worthy charity—anything to keep her mind off her mounting woes. But to dull the almost constant emotional pain of losing a son and a husband, Kathi resorted to political activism, drugs, alcohol, and promiscuous relationships in her nonwaitressing hours, ignoring her son and his needs.

"I thought for a time that I'd finally begun to live the high life. I spent money as if it grew on trees. I stayed up until all hours of the night carousing. I dabbled in cocaine and mescaline. I acted as if I was invincible—as if there were no tomorrow. I practically ignored my son—I was almost entirely self-absorbed."

Then she got pregnant.

"At first, I was entirely unconcerned," she recalled later. "I simply made an appointment for an abortion at the local Planned Parenthood clinic." But that was a big mistake. "The procedure was hellishly painful. But the psychological torture I went through was worse—for the next several weeks, all I could think about was Aaron. That was when I woke up—as if from some kind of a stupor. I felt empty, betrayed, and alone."

That was when she began to drink for consolation. "At first, it was just a few beers or a glass of wine at night. But before long, I was hitting the bottle pretty hard."

When her work began to suffer, Kathi sought help—first from the medical director at Planned Parenthood, later from a psychiatrist. "They gave me some tranquilizers and listened to me ramble, but they never really gave me anything tangible. They never really gave me any help. In the end, I just decided, to hell with it. To hell with it all."

Kathi wound up in the Riverside Clinic, a small Christian rehabilitation center in New York's upper west side that specializes in indigent women. "I just woke up one day in a welfare hotel and realized that I was on the road to becoming one of those shopping bag ladies. I was a total mess."

But if she was a mess, Alex was worse.

At thirteen, Alex was already showing signs of rebellion. He joined a neighborhood gang and got involved with drugs and petty crime, failing in school—primarily because he rarely went to class.

Kathi checked herself into the Riverside program and began the long and arduous task of returning to the mainstream. But Alex was unresponsive to any of the programs available at the center. When he turned fifteen, he left home altogether—by that time sporting a rap sheet longer than his painfully thin arms.

"I'm still bitter," Kathi admitted. "And that's something I'll have to continue to deal with. I know that it was my own foolishness that got me and my son into trouble. The drugs, the alcohol, the promiscuity, the irresponsible lifestyle and all. But even so, it seems to me that women have been led down the primrose path. We've been sold a bill of goods. We've fought so hard to be 'liberated.' To be 'equal.' And here to find out, many of the things that were supposed to bring us 'liberation' have only earned us more pain and more heartache. I wish to God that—well, I wish that I'd just known then what I know today. I feel so stupid that I fell for it. And I feel used—used by Jake, used by the system, and used by this crazy culture."

Martin LaTallia, director of the Riverside Clinic said that Kathi wasn't just venting her anger or shifting the blame for her own foolish mistakes—she had indeed been used. "Fifty years ago a situation like Kathi's simply could not have existed. But the social revolution ushered in over the past two or three decades 'equalized' our institutions and expectations to such a degree that virtually all the social support systems designed to preserve our families and protect women were removed. You could almost say that the family has come under siege."[2]

The Family Revolution

The family is the moral and institutional foundation upon which nearly all human relations are built. It is central to virtually every social endeavor from education to governance, from economics to spirituality, from the care of the aged to the conserving of the earth. The family is the institution that is most effective in solving the problems of poverty, sickness, delinquency, and crisis.

No matter how benevolent, no matter how philanthropic, and no matter how altruistic a government social service agency may be, it can never hope to match the personal intimacy of a family. There is no replacement for the close ties between family members.

> *The family is the original Department of Health, Education and Welfare.*
> —William J. Bennett

And yet, we act as if the family is an unimportant entity and expect the government and its utopian leanings to save our culture. In response to our misguided demands, social spending by the government has increased fivefold in the last thirty years. Inflation-adjusted spending for the vast plethora of social service programs has increased 630 percent, while spending for its sundry educational programs has increased 225 percent.[3] But instead of helping matters, virtually every dollar poured into those programs has only made matters worse. The cure has turned out to be worse than the disease.

Though the grandiose failure of the modern government-sponsored social engineers has been glaringly obvious for more than a decade—fully documented with reams of empirical data—their desire to supplant and succeed the family remains undeterred. In fact, they are more powerful, more influential, and more determined than ever.

> *The contention that the civil government should at its option intrude into and exercise control over the family and the household is a great and pernicious error.*
>
> —Vincenzo Pecci

The utopian vision of society that has so dramatically undermined the family and the mediating institutions around it was spawned by a peculiar and innovative worldview. It was a system of thought rooted in the superiority—even the supremacy—of science over every other discipline or concern. Most social scientists, activists, engineers, and experts believed a fantastic world could be expected in the days just ahead because the sovereign prerogative of science would, no doubt, make short work of curing every cultural ill, correcting every irrational thought, and subverting every cantankerous disturbance. They firmly believed that there was no obstacle too great, no objection too considerable, and no resistance too substantial to restrain the onward and upward march of the scientific evolution of human society.

That kind of unswerving confidence in the good providence of industry and technology gave its adherents a conceited certainty about their forecasts and predictions. As H.G. Wells, one of the leading lights of such sanguine futurism, asserted: "For some of us moderns, who have been touched with the spirit of science, prophesying is almost a habit of mind. Science is very largely analysis aimed at forecasting. The test of any scientific law is our verification of its anticipations. The scientific training develops the idea that whatever is going to happen is really here now—if only one could see it. And when one is taken by surprise, the tendency is not to say with the untrained man, 'Now, who'd ha' thought it?' but 'Now, what was it we overlooked?' Everything that has ever existed or that will ever exist is here—for anyone who has eyes to see. But some of it demands eyes of superhuman penetration."[4]

Science was a kind of new secular predestination. It not only affirmed what could be, it confirmed what would be. And more, it discerned what should be. Scientific experts were thus not only the caretakers of the future, they were the guardians of Truth. They were a kind of superhuman elite—not at all unlike Plato's philosopher-kings—who ruled the untrained masses with a firm but beneficent hand in order to realize the high ideals of progress. Thus, science had to become an instrument of social transformation. It had to be harnessed with the idealism of the far-sighted elite. That meant science had to be necessarily intermingled with ideology. It had to be wielded by the intellectual elite as a tool for the preordained task of human and cultural engineering. It had to be politicized.

Thus, in the early days of the twentieth century, science and millenarian politics were woven together into a crazy quilt of idealism, fanaticism, and ambition. According to Paul Johnson: "With the decline of clerical power in the nineteenth century, a new kind of mentor emerged to fill the vacuum and capture the ear of society. The secular intellectual might be deist, skeptic, or atheist. But he was just as ready as any pontiff or presbyter to tell mankind how to conduct its affairs."[5]

This new breed of prophet, priest, and king brought a tragic compulsion to his task of remaking the world in which he lived: "He proclaimed from the start, a special devotion to the interests of humanity and an evangelical duty to advance them by his teaching. He brought to this self-appointed task a far more radical approach than his clerical predecessors. He felt himself bound by no corpus of revealed religion. The collective wisdom of the past, the legacy of tradition, the prescriptive codes of ancestral experience existed to be selectively followed or wholly rejected entirely as his own good sense might decide. For the first time in human history, and with growing confidence and audacity, men arose to assert that they could diagnose the ills of society and cure them with their own unaided intellects."[6]

As a result, this motley band of social engineers marshaled little more than their wits in their attempts at reinventing humankind—a task no less arduous and no less ludicrous than reinventing the wheel. The result was predictably deleterious.

Ultimately the new world order of these expert futurists was dashed against the hard reality of history. The sad experience of the twentieth century—two devastating world wars, unnumbered holo-causts and genocides, the fierce tyrannies of communism's evil empire, and the embarrassing foibles of liberalism's welfare state—ultimately exposed its high-flying ideals as the noisome eccentricities they were.

Despite history's stern rebuke though, there are still a few die-hard devotees of this ever-hopeful worldview at work in our society. Their chant is rather ragged and shop-worn, but their influence has not yet disappeared altogether. According to historian William Gairdner, they are intent on making one last-ditch effort to usher in their utopia:

> The legions of well-intentioned but smug, educated
> elites have agreed in advance to reject thousands of years
> of inherited wisdom, values, habit, custom, and insight
> and replace this heritage with their official utopian vision
> of the perfect society. They are the progressives, and they

can be found in every political party. Trained as scientific, or logical rationalists, these social utopians haughtily treat all social or moral traditions and conventions as arbitrary, rather than as venerable repositories of indispensable social, family, and religious values. They despise natural authority, especially of a local or family variety, and they want to replace it with a sufficiently homogenous state power to bring about their coercive social dreamland. So with a government wage or grant in one hand and a policy whip in the other, they set about forcibly aligning individuals and customs with their dangerously narrow vision, then clamor after ever greater funding and ever more progressive legislation for the education or socialization of the people.[7]

Despite their best efforts, they will fail, of course—just as they always have in the past. The fact is, science is not infallible. Society is not perfectible. Utopia is not attainable, though attempts at it may surface again and again because "there is evidently a kind of thinking that rejoices in setting up a social objective which has no relation to the individual. Men are prepared to sacrifice their private dignity and happiness to an abstract social ideal, and without asking whether the social ideal produces the welfare of any individual man whatsoever."[8]

As history has shown, the utopian social revolution backfired. We would do well to remember its demise and "employ a certain skepticism even at the expense of the Cult of Science . . . which looks innocent and disinterested, but really is not either." Not that we need to be resistant to technological progress so much as resistant to the crass and inhuman humanism that can accompany scientific advances, aware that "a way of life that omits or de-emphasizes the more spiritual side of existence is necessarily disastrous to all phases of life."[9]

Meanwhile, the effect on families—the real mainstays of our society and our greatest reasons for hope in the days ahead—has been tragic. And worse, the most vulnerable members of our families have suffered the most.

࿇

The Feminization of Poverty

Most of the revolutionary attempts at social engineering have been undertaken, ostensibly, in an effort to improve the lot of women and children in our society. Their effect has been precisely the opposite, and that has contributed to our growing culture of violence.

Economist Sylvia Ann Hewlett has argued in her groundbreaking critique *A Lesser Life: the Myth of Women's Liberation in America* that "modern American women suffer immense economic vulnerability. They have less economic security than their mothers did."[10] A bevy of serious studies, articles, and books have recently demonstrated beyond any shadow of a doubt that social engineering has done much more harm than good.[11] As the *Atlantic Monthly* boldly asserted in a recent cover story, "American women have been sold a bill of goods."[12] Instead of making life easier, or better, or even more just for women, the sundry programs of social engineering have made it harder, worse, and more unjust. They have broken down traditional family structures. They have contributed to epidemic irresponsibility. They have diminished courtesy, respect, and commitment. They have opened a Pandora's box of social ills not the least of which is the progressive impoverishment of the very women it was supposed to liberate.

Evidence of the feminization of poverty everywhere abounds. Seventy percent of today's women in the labor force work out of economic necessity.[13] More often than not, they are single, widowed, or divorced. And more often than not, they are poor. A full 77 percent of this nation's poverty is now borne by women and their children.[14]

The number of poor families headed by men has declined over the last fifteen years by more than 25 percent. Meanwhile, the number of women who headed families below the government's official poverty line increased an alarming 38 percent.[15] Thus today, one in three families headed by women is poor, compared with only one in ten headed by men and a mere one in nineteen headed by two parents.[16]

According to a report of the National Advisory Council on Economic Opportunity, "All other things being equal, if the proportion of the poor in female-householder families were to continue to increase at the same rate as it did over the last two decades, the poverty population would be composed almost solely of women and their children before the year 2000." As it stands today, just over half of all welfare recipients, three-fourths of all Medicare patients, and one fifth of all the homeless are women.[17]

Virtually every plank of our revolutionary social platform has backfired, precipitating a social and economic catastrophe of astounding proportions for American women and their children. Even its idealistic attempts to reform such things as divorce laws and equality in the workplace have only spawned disastrous second- and third-order consequences.

The Divorce Disaster

For instance, social utopians have fought long and hard to have divorce statutes in America follow "gender-neutral" rules—rules designed to treat men and women "equally." In 1970, California capitulated to their demands and introduced the no-fault divorce. Before that time every state required "fault-based grounds for divorce." Some kind of marital fault had to be demonstrated—be it adultery, abandonment, abuse, or cruelty—before a divorce could be granted. The California law changed all that. Within ten years every state but South Dakota and Illinois had followed California's lead.

The practical result of this legal and marital revolution was that divorced women, especially older homemakers and mothers of young children, were deprived of the legal and financial protections that they had traditionally been provided. More often than not, that translated into economic deprivation. According to Lenore J. Weitzman in her book *The Divorce Revolution: The Unexpected Social and Economic Consequences for Women and Children in America*, "on the average, divorced women and the minor children in their households experience a 73 percent decline in their standard of living in the first year after divorce. Their former husbands, in contrast, experience a 42 percent rise in their standard of living." Thus, argues Weitzman, "the major social result of the divorce law revolution is the systematic impoverishment of divorced women and their children. They have become the new poor."[18]

In 1940, one out of every six marriages ended in divorce. Fifty years later, just over 50 percent of all marriages ended in divorce. And demographers are now estimating that by the year 2000, the figure might increase another 16 to 20 percent.[19] With no-fault divorce laws in place, depriving women of alimony, child custody support, or appropriate property settlements, we can expect the feminization of poverty to continue to escalate exponentially.

Workplace Woes

Equality in the workplace was another of the grand schemes of the social planners. It sounded like a good idea. It seemed as if it were the only fair thing to do. After all, who can reasonably argue against "equal pay for equal work?" Equalize the workplace, the experts argued, "and women will have better opportunity."

Sadly, they were wrong.

Equality in the workplace has ironically worked against women in innumerable ways. "Besides the loss of the social advantages that chivalry has traditionally afforded women," says business analyst Hardin Caplin, "the equalization of working conditions and benefits has stripped them of certain maternity-leave options, sick-child allowances, and day care considerations."[20]

"All the special benefits, allowances, and considerations that women once had in the workplace have been eliminated in the name of equality," Richard Levine, professor of social economics at Midwestern University confirmed. "But equality in wages has never materialized, probably because without those benefits, allowances, and considerations women are perceived as risk liabilities; they are perceived as less reliable than their male peers."[21]

Equality then, has been a two-edged sword, slashing at traditional women's benefits and their wage scale. The terrible economic liability is all too evident. Since 1960 the number of women in the workplace has more than doubled. Fully 47 percent of the U.S. labor force is now female. Even so, the gap between male and female earnings has only narrowed one percent in the last half century.[22] According to Sylvia Hewlett, "On average, a woman with four years of college still earns less than a male high school dropout."[23]

Employers attempt to justify the wage gap, saying that whereas men can be counted on to pursue career goals regardless of family circumstances, women are 70 percent more likely to quit mid-career to tend to some crisis at home.[24] "Maternity leaves, sick child allowances, and day care considerations once provided employers with a bit of insurance against the permanent loss of women employees," says Caplin. "But now with equalization and the removal of these special women's benefits, employers simply can't be sure that women will be a good return on their investment."[25]

According to Thomas Sowell, "after several years of 'women's liberation', laws and lawsuits . . . women are now almost up to where they had been nearly half a century earlier."[26] Almost, but not quite.

Clearly, the struggle for equality has wrought more inequality than ever before. "Whenever we attempt to muddy the distinctions— the God-given distinctions—between men and women, it is always the women who ultimately lose," argued nineteenth-century Christian Distributist author Peyton Moore.[27] Moore spoke with prophetic clarity. The utopian social revolution has backfired.

The Ills of Health Reform

But as bad as the record of the social revolution has been in the arena of divorce laws and in the workplace, it has been worse in women's health. Its programs and policies are often lauded as "the bulwark of women's issues."[28] In fact, they may well be the greatest contributing factors in the demise of protection and security for women today.

The experts were instrumental in ushering in a sexual revolution in our time. Sloganeering for "free love," "sex without commitment," "recreational sex," "alternative lifestyle sex," and "casual sex," the utopian social engineers helped create a new sexual ecology that has fundamentally altered American society. As a result, sex outside of the sacred confines of marriage is now considered "normal."[29]

There have been innumerable unexpected, unintended, and unwanted results. Teen pregnancies. Family disintegration. Women-headed homes. Illegitimacy. Male irresponsibility.

According to the Department of Health and Human Services National Center for Health Statistics, today as many as 65 percent of all African-American children are born out of wedlock.[30] In 1940 only about 15 percent were. In some communities, that percentage is even higher: 80 to 90 percent. In 1965, only one out of four African-American families was headed by a woman.[31] Today more than half are headed by females.

This crisis of illegitimacy is not restricted to minority communities. Nearly 14 percent of all white births were to teenagers.[32] The birth rate for unwed white women rose by 25 percent in the decade from 1969 to 1979 and another 12 percent in the decade that followed.[33]

The sexual revolution spawned a situation where men freely accepted the pleasures and privileges of intimacy without having to accept any of its responsibilities. Women were left holding the baby. Literally.

And then there is the problem of sexually transmitted diseases.

The utopian social revolutionaries loudly announced their efforts to battle against sexually transmitted diseases. But their commitment to promiscuous sex—to say nothing of their institutional policies and programs—actually belies that fact.

The truth is, the experts' efforts have been tragically counterproductive in the fight against sexually transmitted diseases. They have become veritable Typhoid Marys, actually encouraging the spread of syphilis, gonorrhea, chlamydia, herpes, hepatitis, granuloma, chancroid, and even AIDS. Besides the fact that they constantly exhort clients at "family planning" clinics to flaunt a ribald and irresponsible promiscuity, they continually promote an alarmingly "unsafe" exercise of promiscuity. For instance, 80 percent of Planned Parenthood's clients receive non-barrier contraceptives, and 88 percent of those who previously practiced "safe sex" are dissuaded from continuing. [34]

Admittedly, barrier devices such as condoms offer only limited protection against venereal infection.[35] Due to in-use mechanical failure—leaks, breaks, tears, slippage, and spillage—their effectiveness has been estimated to be at best 82 percent.[36] But the Pill offers no protection whatsoever. Neither do IUDs, diaphragms, spermicides, contraceptive sponges, Depo-Provera, Norplant, RU-486, or any of the other non-barrier birth control devices that today's experts favor. Worse, recent studies indicate that not only do these methods fail to guard against venereal infection, they may actually enhance the risks.[37] "Apparently," says economic demographer Robert Ruff, the utopian experts believe that "safe sex is a lot less important than free sex."[38]

Another of the revolution's utopian disasters has been abortion-on-demand.

Claiming to protect a woman's right to choose and to provide safe and legal abortion services, the social revolution was supposed to remove the specter of dangerous back-alley abortions from our land. But that is hardly the case. Sadly, the specter remains, darker and more ominous than ever before. The truth is, many of the same butchers who ran the old illegal back-alley operations have simply moved uptown to ply their grisly trade legally.[39] The 1973 *Roe v. Wade* decision did nothing to change that.

There is no such thing as a "safe and legal" abortion. Legal, yes. Safe, no way.[40]

Recently the Centers for Disease Control conducted a study of maternal deaths and discovered that abortion is now the sixth most common cause. The results of the study, released in the journal *Obstetrics and Gynecology*, admitted that those abortion-related deaths may be under-reported by as much as 50 percent.[41]

According to a Johns Hopkins University study, nearly 20 percent of all mid-trimester abortions result in serious genital tract infections. And a study conducted by two UCLA obstetrical and gynecological professors concluded that "abortion can be a killer," due to "pelvic abscess, perforation of the uterus, and sometimes also of the bowel." But even if such infections and abscesses do not prove to be fatal, they can cause serious and permanent medical complications. According to one physician, writing in the *British Journal of Venereal Disease*, "infection in the womb and tubes often does permanent damage. The fallopian tube is a fragile organ, a very tiny bore tube. If infection injures it, it often seals shut. The typical infection involving these organs is pelvic inflammatory disease, or PID." This condition affects nearly 15 percent of all those who submit to induced abortion.[42]

Other medical complications of abortion include sterility, which happens to as many as 25 percent of all women receiving mid-trimester abortions; hemorrhaging, which occurs in nearly 10 percent of all cases requiring transfusions; viral hepatitis, which occurs in 10 percent of all those transfused; embolism, which appears in about 4 percent of all cases; cervical laceration, cardiorespiratory arrest, acute kidney failure, and amniotic fluid embolus, which happen in as many as 42 percent of all Prostaglandin abortions.[43]

As a result of these complications, women in America have seen a massive increase in the cost of medical care. While the average cost of normal health maintenance for men has increased nearly 12 percent over the last eight years due to inflation, the average cost for women has skyrocketed a full 27 percent.[44]

The great vision the coercive social engineers conceived has utterly failed.

Kathi Tannenbaum knows that now. She learned the hard way.

"When Jake left me, I figured we'd be okay. I figured life would go on. I figured the courts would make him take care of me and Alex. Later I figured my feminist activism would make things right. Then I figured I could just drown all my troubles and disappointments in a pool of illicit pleasure. But, I figured wrong."[45]

Instead of advancing the cause of women and their children, the utopian revolution set them back more than half a century. It feminized poverty. It laid siege to the family. As author Mary Pride has concluded, "Today's women are the victims of the second biggest con game in history—the first was when the serpent persuaded Eve she needed to upgrade her lifestyle and 'become like God.'"[46]

The Breakdown of the Family and Crime

The siege on the family has had a direct effect on crime—and particularly, juvenile crime. Robert Bork has persuasively argued that "the United States has surely never before experienced the social chaos and the accompanying personal tragedies that have become routine today; high rates of crime and low rates of punishment, high rates of illegitimate births subsidized by welfare, and high rates of family dissolution through no-fault divorce. These pathologies are recent, and it is now widely accepted that they are related to one another."[47]

The statistics make this all too evident. More than 80 percent of all violent juvenile offenders are the products of broken homes. Nearly 70 percent live in single-parent households. As many as 90 percent have suffered some sort of physical, sexual, or emotional abuse.[48]

Again, according to Bork: "There is no longer any doubt that communities with many single parents, whether because of divorce or out-of-wedlock births, display much higher rates of crime, drug use, school dropouts, voluntary unemployment, etc. Nor is there any doubt that the absence of a father is damaging not only to the unwed mother but to the prospects of the children."[49]

One recent study found that when families are disrupted by divorce, illegitimacy, or domestic violence, teens are sixty-four times more likely to get involved in criminal activity. They are seventy times more likely to engage in illicit sex. They are seventy-four times more likely to abuse drugs or alcohol. And they are fifty-six times more likely to join a gang.[50]

> *For good or for ill, the estate of the family will most assuredly predetermine the estate of all of the rest of the culture.*
>
> —Patrick Henry

Gangs are, in fact, a kind of substitute family structure. They offer rootless children the opportunity to have the kind of structure, community, commitment, accountability, and sense of identity that healthy families normally provide. In the absence of healthy families, the need for those kinds of human bonds do not disappear. Children search for an outlet that will satisfy them. As a result, those children are drawn into the web of violence, crime, and devastation that naturally accompanies gang culture.

According to Karl Zinmeister in a report for the American Enterprise Institute: "There is a mountain of scientific evidence showing that when families disintegrate, children end up with intellectual, physical, and emotional scars that persist for life. We talk about the drug crisis, the education crisis, and the problem of teen pregnancy and juvenile crime. But all these ills trace back predominantly to one source: broken families."[51]

We must now turn our efforts and attentions to supporting and healing our families. Obviously, if the epidemic of violence in our communities is to be arrested in any measure—if we are to keep our children from killing children—then we must strengthen the bonds of family life. We must make strong families our priority again. We must put families, not science, first.

7

In the Name of Education

'*Tis education forms the tender mind. Just as the twig is bent the tree's inclined.*[1]

—Thomas Fessenden

Shannon Wright's first instinct was to step between her students and the danger that rained down on them from the low ridge just above the schoolyard. When gunfire cut through the youngsters at Westside Middle School, Wright was just a couple of feet away from the doorway. But instead of ducking back inside the building, she grabbed a little girl and pulled her out of the line of fire. Seconds later, the selfless woman who had always dreamed of being a teacher, crumpled to the ground, shot in the stomach.

Emma Pittman, the student she had just saved, could only watch in horror. "All I really remember was that she fell, and I started to run," Emma said later. "She went 'uhmmmmmmff,' sort of a soft sound, with pain. She just fell straight down."[2]

A local girl, Wright had attended the Westside schools, where she was a popular cheerleader. She got her teaching certificate at Arkansas State University in Jonesboro. She met her husband, Mitch, in college. She was a dedicated wife and mother—her little boy, Zane, was her pride and joy. But she was also a dedicated teacher. She was perpetually exuberant and cheerful. She had pet names for almost all of her students and composed silly jingles to help them remember their grammar. "We were always laughing at her jokes," recalled Emma.[3]

Her dedication knew no bounds. Alas, she paid the ultimate price for her students.

A few hours after she was struck, Shannon Wright died at St. Bernard's Hospital of massive internal bleeding—but not before saying to the doctors attending her, "Tell Mitch that I love him and I love Zane and to take care of my baby."[4]

She was universally heralded as a hero. But undoubtedly she would have found the outpouring of grief and the tributes to her dedication rather odd—perhaps even a bit disconcerting. After all, she was a teacher. She wouldn't have dreamed of being anything else or doing anything else.

America's classroom teachers are the unheralded heroes of our land. Every day they sacrifice their self-interest for the sake of our children. Often working long hours in difficult circumstances with less than adequate resources and even less thanks, our teachers have more often than not set aside their personal ambitions, career opportunities, and concerns to mentor the next generation of young men and women.

It is tragic that it takes the loss of someone as remarkable as Shannon Wright to realize our great debt to these public servants.

It is also tragic that their sacrifice is more often than not obscured from public view by the looming crisis in public education. For all their hard work and selfless commitment, our schools face tremendous challenges today. And they are challenges that may even aggravate the spreading culture of violence among our children, thus putting teachers and students alike in jeopardy—as Shannon Wright lamentably discovered.

⌘

Suffer the Children

"A nation at risk." That is the United States Department of Education's declaration on our country's educational status . . . and with good reason.[5] The once-lauded quality of our public educational system has been in a steady decline for nearly three decades.[6] In many places all across the country, teacher competency is down. Administrative effectiveness is down. Student advancement is down. Test scores are down. Nearly everything to do with our public school system is down—everything, that is, except crime, violence, drug abuse, illicit sex, and the cost to taxpayers.[7]

As many as 90 million adults in this country are functionally illiterate. An additional 35 million are alliterate—they can read a few basics with difficulty.[8] Standard Achievement Test (SAT) score comparisons reveal an almost unbroken decline from 1963 to the present.[9] Average verbal scores have fallen more than fifty points, and mathematics scores have dropped nearly forty points. The United States now ranks forty-ninth in literacy among the 158 countries of the United Nations.[10]

Nearly 40 percent of all high school seniors cannot draw inferences from written material; only one-fifth can write a persuasive essay; and less than one-third can solve an arithmetic problem requiring multiple steps. Thirty-eight percent cannot locate the Mississippi River on a map of North America, 35 percent cannot find the Rocky Mountains, and 42 percent cannot identify their own home state.[11]

One study found that 25 million high school graduates cannot correctly identify the United States on an outline map of the world, 44 million cannot find the Pacific Ocean, and some 61 million are unable to come within 500 miles of locating the nation's capital.[12] Another study revealed that nearly one-third of all graduating high school seniors cannot identify the Declaration of Independence as marking the formal break between the American colonies and Great Britain, 28 percent do not know that Columbus discovered America in 1492—believing that the event occurred sometime between 1750 and 1850, and 32 percent are unable to name more than three past presidents.[13]

Nearly half of all Americans are so poorly prepared in basic mathematics and literacy that they can't perform such relatively simple tasks as calculating the price difference between two items at the grocery store or filling out a job application at a fast-food restaurant.[14]

A recent study by the National Endowment for the Humanities saw these dismal statistics as a harbinger of national decline and disintegration: "Knowledge of the ideas that have molded us and the ideals that have mattered to us function as a kind of civic glue. By failing to transmit these ideas and ideals from one generation to the next, we risk dissolution of the bonds that unite us as a nation and as a free people."[15]

Society is quick to put the blame on the government-run school system, as evidenced by a recent *Washington Post* poll which showed that only about 14 percent of all Americans have a great deal of faith in public education. As a result, enrollment in private schools has increased more than 60 percent in the past two decades.[16] Ironically, public school teachers have themselves heavily contributed to the boost in enrollment of private schools since many of them have taken their own children out of the public system.[17]

One would think that one of the most extensive and expensive school systems the world has ever seen would have better results.[18] Spending—in inflation adjusted dollars—has increased some 400 percent per pupil in the past thirty years. Teacher salaries have

> *The philosophy of the classroom in one generation will be the philosophy of government in the next.*
>
> —Abraham Lincoln

more than doubled—again in inflation adjusted dollars. And the per capita number of support personnel has nearly quadrupled. Education has, in fact, become the second largest industry in the nation, spending more than $250 trillion every year, with nearly 3 million teachers and administrators.[19] And yet, more than 45 percent of the products of that system cannot even read the front page of the morning newspaper.[20]

According to a report from the National Commission on Excellence in Education: "If an unfriendly foreign power had attempted to impose on America the mediocre educational system, it could not have devised one worse than the one we presently have."[21]

How could this have happened?

❧

State of the Union

According to a recent *Forbes* magazine profile, the National Education Association (NEA) is "the worm in the American education apple." *Forbes* further stated that the "public may be only dimly aware of it, but the union's growing power has exactly coincided with the dismal spectacle of rising spending on education producing deteriorating results."[22]

Syndicated columnist James Kilpatrick agrees, noting that the "NEA in recent years has come to embody every single cause that has contributed to the crisis that threatens our public schools."[23]

It has not been our dedicated teachers who have brought on this educational crisis. It has not been our committed principals, administrators, and school board members. Instead, it has been the steady politicalization of our schools by a handful of union organizers. It has been the NEA.

Founded in 1857 by representatives of several state teachers associations, the NEA is currently the country's largest labor union. With a membership now approaching 3 million, an annual combined budget of $500 million, and a standing political war chest of nearly $20 million, the union is one of the most powerful forces in American life today. It is the largest single interest group lobbying in Washington.[24] In several states, it wields more influence than all of the other major special interests combined. It has the largest and richest political action committee. It is the biggest broker of group insurance benefits. And it is the major ideological force in more than 90 percent of some 16,000 local public school districts throughout the nation.[25]

For nearly thirty years, the union has maintained a smothering monopoly over every aspect of America's government-run educational system—from the content of the curriculum to the proposal of budgets, from the design of facilities to the administration of bureaucracies, from classroom methodologies to teacher salaries, from political reform to regulatory control.[26]

But its appetite for new kingdoms to conquer remains unsated. According to author and educator Phoebe Courtney, the union is not satisfied with controlling public education: "It wants complete control over all American education—private as well as public. It has vowed to bring private education under its control through teacher certification and state accreditation laws."[27]

To that end, the union has launched a series of initiatives aimed at consolidating its power nationwide by:

- Working diligently to promote the nationalization of educational standards to ensure complete uniformity in teaching content, methodology, administration, and outcome
- Spending millions of dollars fighting against school choice measures that would allow parents to choose the best schooling options for their children according to their own criteria
- Fighting for either the elimination or the strict regulation of homeschooling—in some states even going so far as to establish "enforcement units" to identify and seek prosecution of parents that homeschool their children without government approval or certification
- Attempting to stymie any and all educational reform—particularly when that reform involves diversifying the educational options available to taxpayers and parents
- Lobbying for centralization of control of the financing of education—recommending that the current system of local financing be scrapped for a federal system.[28]

In 1967 Sam Lambert, the union's executive secretary, predicted that the "National Education Association will become a political power second to no other special interest group . . . we will organize this profession from top to bottom into logical operational units that can move swiftly and effectively and with power unmatched by any other organized group in the nation."[29]

By all counts, that prophecy has been fulfilled.

Initially called the National Teacher's Association, the union was largely a home office for the federated state education associations during its first seventy-five years or so of existence. It engaged in some modest research, lobbied state legislators in support of higher pay and better retirement benefits, and promoted progressive methodological ideas of education.

According to educational pioneer Samuel Blumenfeld: "The NEA was little more than a discussion club for superintendents, state education officers, and college presidents. Its conventions were commercially self-serving, philosophically stimulating but politically inconsequential."[30]

In 1962, a dramatic change occurred: the NEA wed its modest commercial interests and haute educational fashions with the organizational leverage of the labor movement—transforming from a loosely affiliated professional association to a full-fledged union. Since that time, the vast proportion of its efforts and expenditures have been focused on the progressive politicalization of the educational system. Consequently, the urgent task of improving the schools has taken a backseat to the promotion and consolidation of the union's power. Today, less than 4 percent of the union's vast annual budget is actually spent on instruction and professional development. All the rest is poured into maintaining and expanding the union's dominating control over the American educational debacle.[31]

Scott Thompson, executive director of the National Association of Secondary School Principals, has said, "The NEA no longer contributes to the improvement of teaching and learning for students. It looks after the narrow interests of its members rather than after the broader interests of its constituency."[32]

The union even admits as much: "The major purpose of our association is not the education of children, it is or ought to be the extension and preservation of our members' rights. We earnestly care about the kids learning, but that is secondary to the other goals."[33]

Thus, Congressman John Ashbrook was hardly exaggerating when he quipped, "Any observer of the current scene has to realize that the NEA's priorities these days break down like this: power first, politics second, and education last."[34]

The Politicization of Education

"If I become president, you'll be my partners," declared candidate Bill Clinton to the NEA Candidate Screening Panel in 1991. "I won't forget who brought me to the White House."[35]

He kept his promise.

According to Dan Alexander, a Washington-based educational analyst, the NEA "has become the single most dominant force in the national Democratic party." Nearly a quarter of the floor delegates at the party's last five national conventions were members or officials of the NEA.[36] About 20 percent of the delegates Clinton needed for his nomination came from the rank and file of the union. And close to one-eighth of his campaign budget came from the union's political coffers.[37]

In 1978, that kind of faithful zealotry for the Democratic party was rewarded when Jimmy Carter created the massive Department of Education—a goal of the union since its establishment more than a century earlier.[38] Afterward, one official boasted, "We are the only union with our own Cabinet department."[39]

It was rewarded again with the first Clinton budget, which pledged a 22 percent increase in the federal funding and control of local schools.[40]

During each of the past three congressional elections, the union has spent more than $2.5 million supporting various candidates and causes—an overwhelming majority of them from the extreme left of the political spectrum. Despite the fact that two-thirds of all teachers describe their political philosophy as "conservative," militant left-wing political activism has become the backbone of their union.[41] Indeed, a survey of its policy positions bears that fact out all too clearly:

- The NEA is at the vanguard of the "political correctness" movement—from multiculturalism and inclusive language, to speech codes and hate crimes.
- It has embraced the entire feminist agenda—including abortion-on-demand, value-free kindergarten-through-twelfth-grade sex education, school-based sex clinics, and quota hiring and advancement standards.
- It has joined forces with militant homosexual groups in pressing for special-status legislative protections and condom give-aways in the schools,[42] and endorsed the most recent gay-rights march on Washington.[43]
- It opposes school prayer or any other demonstration of faith in the public sector.
- It opposes tuition tax credits.
- It has actively opposed conservative appointments to the Supreme Court from Clement Haynesworth and Harold Carswell to Robert Bork and Clarence Thomas.
- It has consistently opposed drug and alcohol sobriety testing for students.

- It has supported the right of schools to bypass parental authority in securing sexuality counseling, procedures, and services.[44]

Those who disagree with the NEA's monolithic liberal agenda are labeled by the union as "chronic tax resisters, congenital reactionaries, dangerous witch hunters, energized super patriots, wayward dogma peddlers, and vitriolic race-haters." According to former school principal and conservative educational lobbyist, Michael Harlinson: "Though it constantly harps on a gospel of tolerance and diversity, the NEA is fierce in its denunciation of any and all political opposition. It anathematizes and criminalizes its critics with an intensity that even the Mafia could admire."[45]

According to Phyllis Schlafly, the union is hardly interested in serious issues of education. Instead, its words and deeds point to "an arrogance of power, a compulsion to control the minds and behavior of children, and a pervasive hostility toward parents."[46]

No wonder our schools are in such awful shape despite the best efforts of our dedicated classroom teachers.

The Little Red Schoolhouse

The National Education Association's primary philosophical guru was John Dewey, an educator from Columbia University. Dewey believed that the primary purpose of education was the promotion of "socialization." Thus he wrote, "Not knowledge or information, but self-realization is the goal." He believed that "the mind is not the property of the individual, but of humanity."[47]

The educational methodology that he worked out discouraged "abstract learning" and encouraged "social skills" through "social studies." Schools thus became "psycho-therapeutic socializers for the harmony of the wider community."[48]

Because the union threw its full weight behind Dewey's approach to teaching and learning, the entire government-run educational system gradually turned its attentions away from academic achievement and toward a bevy of methodological fads:

- It helped to replace phonics with the "look-say" method of teaching reading, which has greatly contributed to the nation's precipitous decline in literacy.

- Its emphasis on "socialization" has resulted in decreased requirements in math and the sciences—again contributing to plunging student competency rates.

- Its attempt to transform teachers into "equippers" has resulted in a massive exodus of qualified teachers from the public school ranks.

- Its opposition to merit raises, teacher competency testing, and recertification standards has resulted in a system that harbors incompetency but fails to reward achievement.

- Its insistence on tenure protections for all government school positions has resulted in incompetent teachers and administrators securing job immutability.[49]

Even the overtly liberal *New Republic* magazine was forced to admit that "nearly every necessary step to high quality American public education is being fought by the NEA."[50]

But it gets worse. The union's most recent fascination is called "Outcome-Based Education." Though the rhetoric of this "school restructuring" plan sounds good enough, the reality is abominably subversive. According to Michael Harlinson, "Every parent wants to achieve certain goals or outcomes for their children at school—they want them to learn to read, to acquire certain math and science skills, and to develop logical and deductive disciplines. But this is not at all what Outcome-Based Education is about. Instead, it is a series of social experiments designed to turn out a certain set of social outcomes—self-esteem, tolerance, sexual responsibility, and value-free consciences. In other words, what the union means by outcomes and what the parents mean by outcomes are quite likely two entirely different things."[51]

As presently constituted, the Outcome-Based Education plan is a nightmare of liberalism run amuck. Objective academic disciplines are replaced by subjective feelings, attitudes, and values. It also calls for a least-common-denominator kind of egalitarian scheme that stifles individual achievement and obscures individual needs. In addition, the plan offers absolutely no method of accountability to students, parents, teachers, or taxpayers—essentially because it includes no objective standards.[52]

> *Do you sometimes have an uneasy suspicion that the product of modern educational methods is less good than he or she might be at disentangling fact from opinion and the proven from the plausible? Although we often succeed in teaching our pupils subjects, we fail lamentably on the whole in teaching them how to think. They learn everything except the art of learning.*
>
> —Dorothy Sayers

Although there has yet to be any empirical study, replicable research, or pilot data to demonstrate that the program works, hundreds of schools have already introduced the restructuring plan. In essence, this untested, irresponsible program has been launched entirely "on faith."[53]

As Harlinson has said, "With its latest hobbyhorse, Outcome-Based Education, the National Education Association has given up all pretense of trying to educate public school children in favor of propagandizing them with pop-psychotherapeutic pap. Instead of teaching them the three R's—reading, writing, and arithmetic, it is enthusiastically indoctrinating them with the four R's—reversionism, revisionism, reprobation, and radicalism."[54]

✁

Whose Values?

Outcome-Based Education is often an overt assault on Christian family values. For example, one teacher's guidebook for New York's controversial Outcome-Based Education restructuring plan states: "Teachers of first-graders have an opportunity to give children a healthy sense of identity at an early age. Classes should include references to lesbians and gays in all curricular areas and should avoid exclusionary practices by presuming a person's sexual orientation, reinforcing stereotypes, or speaking of lesbians and gays as 'they' or 'other.' If teachers do not discuss lesbian and gay issues, they are not likely to come up. Children need actual experiences via creative play, books, visitors, etc. in order for them to view lesbians and gays as real people to be respected and appreciated. Educators have the potential to help increase the tolerance and acceptance of the lesbian and gay community."[55]

"Why Johnny Can't Learn About Condoms," an article in the homosexual *Advocate* magazine, vilified "fundamentalist Christians" for opposing homosexual content in Outcome-Based Education: "Public education epitomizes the religious right's problem with non-Christian society. Public schools serve the function of mainstreaming people—making them into decent, tolerant adults. For certain fundamentalists, that makes public schools the enemy, and they have been able to make this case to a lot of other parents."[56]

Apparently, our taxes are being spent on raising children in values alien to the Christian faith—"mainstreamed" by the government through the educational establishment and its attendant bureaucratic machinery. And if you object, you are guilty of "censorship."[57]

This fundamental incongruity in the American tradition of freedom is not some new development in public education. Horace Mann, who is universally recognized as the father of the American public education system, admitted that public schools were needed "as a means for the state to control people."[58] He said: "Great care must be taken to inform and regulate the will of the people."[59] Thus, the National Education Association's tactic of getting at children through the public education system is as old as government-run schools are.

The proponents of Outcome-Based Education are not merely concerned about passing out tidbits of immoral information, but wish to instill moral—or, more accurately, immoral—beliefs. As one union official forthrightly admitted, "Mere facts and discussion are not enough. They need to be undergirded by a set of values."[60]

Again, this is nothing new. American public education has always been driven by moral values. But Horace Mann's arguments for the public school had almost nothing to do with reading, writing, and arithmetic, but with inculcating children with his version of morality: "Keep children unspotted from the world, that is, uncontaminated by its vices; to train them up to the love of God and the love of man; to make the perfect example of Jesus Christ lovely in their eyes; and to give to all so much of religious instruction *as is compatible with the rights of others and the genius of our government*" (italics mine).[61]

Though he wanted religion in the public school, he was opposed to orthodox Christianity and, instead, wished to promulgate Unitarianism. He did not do this by calling for Unitarianism to be recognized as the official state religion; rather, he simply called for the religious teaching in the schools to be "nonsectarian."

The director of Equal Educational Opportunity for the Commonwealth of Massachusetts, Charles Leslie Glenn Jr., writes:

> Thus, although Mann and the other education reformers may not have intended to promote Unitarianism as a denomination, they were deeply concerned to assure that "liberal religion" would, through the common schools, replace "fanaticism." Were the normal schools some sort of Unitarian conspiracy, then? Only in the sense that they represented the most effective means for the education reformers (themselves mostly but not exclusively "liberal Christians") to develop a supply of teachers who would share their own views about the "pure religion" appropriate to offer as religious instruction in common schools. . . . Orthodox beliefs were not confronted directly, but they were relativized, marginalized. It was by a selective emphasis upon certain elements of Christianity, in a vocabulary familiar from childhood, that the idea was conveyed that these were the real essentials of the faith.[62]

Furthermore, according to Glenn, Mann pioneered subtle methods of centrally controlling education which are still used today: "The collection and interpretation of educational statistics, ostensibly a perfectly neutral activity, had and continues to have the power to define perceptions of the salient strengths and weaknesses of the schools. The recommendation of reading material—and the banning of other material—had and continues to have the power to shape the range of topics that may be taught or discussed, and the framework in which they will be understood. The training—and eventually the certification—of teachers had and continues to have the power to determine what will occur in the classroom, far more than any system of regulation and prescription."

Consequently, according to Christian educator Richard Catherwood, "we are going to have to face the fact that the entire public education scheme was and is flawed. We are going to have to go back to square one—in repentance—and essentially learn how to learn all over again."[63]

A Lifetime of Learning

The English novelist and etymologist J. R. R. Tolkien once told his students that all true education is actually "a kind of never-ending story—a matter of continual beginnings, of habitual fresh starts, of persistent newness." Similarly, his great friend C. S. Lewis said that education is "like a tantalizingly perpetual verandah—the initiation of unending beginnings."[64]

That paradoxical perspective was likewise shared by E. M. Bounds, a southern pastor and theologian of the last century who understood that the past is but a prelude to the future and that the present is necessarily tutelage in an unending process, remarking: "The primer of faith is never closed for the child of God. It's lessons never end. No matter what circumstances may bode, we remain under the bar of instruction forever. Every incident builds upon the last and anticipates the next."[65]

For many, it is sad to say, this uniquely Christian perspective is an entirely foreign worldview—an alien notion, an arcane paradox, an unfathomable mystery. Minds dulled by the smothering conformity of popular culture cannot plumb the depths or explore the breadths of the distinctively Christian virtue of hopeful contentment in the face of perpetual tasks. Thus they rush toward what they think will be the termination of each chapter in their lives. They cannot wait to finish school since graduation is not a commencement for them, but a conclusion. Afterward, they hurry through their lives and careers: they plod impatiently through their work week, anxious for the weekend; they bide their time until vacation; and endure their careers until retirement—always coming to an end of things until, at last, things come to an end.

In the Christian worldview, hopeful contentment in the face of never-ending responsibilities is a virtue that continually breeds anticipation for new beginnings. It is a virtue that provokes us to a fresh confidence in the present as well as in the days yet to come. It is a virtue rooted in an understanding of God's good providence and in the covenant fortunes of His grace.

We Christians who were brought from death to life—from the end of ourselves to the threshold of eternity—understand this. The very essence of the Gospel is that the crucifixion was not the termination of Christ's mediatorial work but the conjunction of two beginnings: the incarnation and the resurrection. It is the pivot of civilization that marks a new creation: "Old things have passed away; behold, all things have become new" (2 Cor. 5:17).

Thus, for example, all talk of education is for us a reminder that we have only just begun to learn. It is an affirmation that though our magnificent heritage has introduced us to the splendid wonders of literature, art, music, history, and science—we have only just been introduced and that a lifelong adventure in these vast arenas still awaits us.

Indeed, the most valuable lessons that education can convey are invariably the lessons that never end. That is actually at the heart of the Christian philosophy of education.

In his introduction to John Henry Newman's brilliant *The Idea of a University*, the renowned educator Leo Brennan asserts that "though we don't have much to show for it, we Americans are enthusiasts for education."[66] He's right. Though there is perhaps an underlying "anti-intellectualism" in a few isolated circles, by and large we Americans—and particularly we American Christians—place a heavy emphasis on the education of our children. We demand good teachers, good textbooks, good facilities, and good supplemental resources. We demand the best of everything academia has to offer. Which makes our profound lack of it—even within the Christian community—all the more ironic.

> *The public schools of today sadly demonstrate an arrogance of power, a compulsion to control the minds and behavior of children, and a pervasive hostility toward parents.*
>
> —Phyllis Schlafly

The problem, says Brennan, is that "we engage in the eminently dubious process of what is barbarously known as standardization." As a result, "we lower our ideals and we smear our philosophy" by playing "the sedulous ape to popular uniformitarian educational fads and fashions."[67]

The only solution, he argues, is to "restore the basic educational ideals and principles" that provoked Christendom's great flowering of culture in the first place: a strident emphasis on serious and diverse reading and the use of classical methodologies, which are to be integrated into the gracious environs of Christian family life.[68]

Sadly, that is not a particularly popular perspective these days. Serious reading, classical content, and familial superintendence are simply not in vogue. They represent archaisms long since left in the dust of time by the new fangled gadgetry of industrial contemporaneity and progressive modernity.

Is it any wonder that despite the best efforts of our dedicated teachers, our schools are often failing in their most basic tasks? And is it any wonder that in this contentiously politicized environment, the already-tense cultural conflicts of our day sadly erupt into violence? Our schools (once the haven of our community standards), our sense of public virtue, and our common commitment to our children have in many places become laboratories for radical social experiments.

But that need not be. We can honor the sacrifices of our dedicated teachers and restore a sense of security in our schools simply by establishing education—not socialization—as the primary purpose of our schools. We can maintain the memory of selfless heroes like Shannon Wright if we would simply recommit ourselves to the future of our children rather than to the future of our agendas.

Education is not an object, a product, or an outcome. It is the fruit of diligence and faithfulness in rightly related individuals. As Susan Schaeffer Macaulay has said, "Education is an adventure that has to do with central themes, not the particular packages a given generation puts them into. It's about people, children, life, and reality."[69]

Education does not have a terminus, a polar extreme, a finish line, an outcome. Instead it is a deposit, an endowment, a promise, and even a small taste of the future. And though that makes it a difficult task, it also makes it a worthwhile task. In his remarkable book *The Moral Sense,* James Q. Wilson drives home that point with great clarity. He claims that "the best things in life" invariably "cost us something."[70] We must sacrifice to attain them, to achieve them, to keep them, even to enjoy them.

That is one of the most important lessons we can learn in life. It is the message that we know we ought to instill in our children: patience, commitment, diligence, constancy, and discipline will ultimately pay off if we are willing to defer gratification long enough for the seeds we have sown to sprout. A flippant, shallow, and imprecise approach to anything—be it sports or academics or the trades or business or marriage—is ultimately self-defeating. It is not likely to satisfy any appetite—at least, not for long. That is the heart and soul of true education.

G. K. Chesterton has sagely observed: "The great intellectual tradition that comes down to us from the past was never interrupted or lost through such trifles as the sack of Rome, the triumph of Attila, or all the barbarian invasions of the Dark Ages. It was lost after the introduction of printing, the discovery of America, the coming of the marvels of technology, the establishment of universal education, and all the enlightenment of the modern world. It was there, if anywhere, that there was lost or impatiently snapped the long thin delicate thread that had descended from distant antiquity; the thread of that unusual human hobby: the habit of thinking."[71]

Perhaps it is time to revive that unusual human hobby—and thus, bring hope and help to a whole new generation sorely in need of both.

Part 3

❧

A BRIGHTER DAY AHEAD

There is only one form of political strategy in which I have any confidence, and that is to try to do the right thing—and sometimes be able to succeed.[1]
—Calvin Coolidge

8

❧

Government against

the People

It is a greater honor to be right than to be president—
or popular . . . for statesmanship consists rather in
removing causes than in punishing or evading
results—thus, it is the rarest of qualities.[1]
                                    —James A. Garfield

Every time a problem arises in our society, we can expect to hear the same litany of responses: "The government needs to do more"; "There ought to be a law"; "The president, or Congress, or the state legislature, or the governor, or the courts must act—and act immediately."

Unfortunately, since it took us quite some time to get into the nationwide mess we currently find ourselves in, it may take us a good while to get out of it. The dilemma of juvenile violence will not be solved by passing a bevy of new laws or by instituting a slew of new programs or by establishing a series of new institutions. Indeed, most of the rash of recent shootings in our nation's schools would not have been prevented even if the most stringent gun control proposals, school security systems, or social engineering plans had been in place.

What we really need are not new and more restrictive laws, stronger and more intrusive regulations, or larger and more comprehensive government agencies. What we need are grassroots renewals of those things that originally made America great. The crux of our current crisis is not economic, educational, institutional, scientific, or political. It is cultural. We have loosed upon our children a world of woe—and we have simultaneously stripped them of every moral and ethical apparatus necessary to deal adequately with that woe.

We are prone to look for the quick fix. We want instant relief for that which ails us. But our long experience with politics ought to be enough to tell us that even if a panacea exists, it probably won't be found in the arena of politics and law.

⌘

The Limitations of Politics

In many ways, Lyndon Johnson was a prototype of the modern politician who lives and breathes politics. He once satirically quipped, "I seldom think of politics more than eighteen hours a day."[2]

The man who succeeded John Kennedy as president of the United States believed that civil government was the most important force in modern life.[3] Thus, political power was everything to him. He honestly could not think of anything more significant in life than the wild and woolly machinations of politics. For him such things defined the character of culture and shaped the temper of society. Unfortunately, he was misguided in his belief.

As syndicated columnist George Will once argued, "There is hardly a page of American history that does not refute the insistence, so characteristic of the political class, on the primacy of politics in the making of history." As a matter of fact, "In a good society, politics is peripheral to much of the pulsing life of the society."[4]

Certainly, politics is important. But it is not all-important.

Many who live and die by the electoral sword will probably be shocked to discover that most of the headline-making events in the political realm today will probably go down in the annals of time as mere backdrops to the real drama of the everyday affairs

> We do not need to get good laws to restrain bad people. We need to get good people to restrain bad laws.
>
> —G. K. Chesterton

of life. As much emphasis as is placed on campaigns, primaries, caucuses, conventions, elections, statutes, laws, policy proposals, legislative initiatives, administrations, surveys, opinion polls, demographic trends, and bureaucratic programs these days, the reality is that the importance of fellow workers, next-door neighbors, close friends, and family members is actually far greater. Political skullduggery—however much it may or may not upset us—is, in the end, rather remote from the things that really matter. Despite all the hype of sensational turns-of-events, the affairs of ordinary people who tend their gardens, raise their children, perfect their trades, and mind their businesses are more important. Just like they always have been. Just like they always will be.

That is one of the great lessons of history. As G. K. Chesterton aptly observed, "The greatest political storm flutters only a fringe of humanity. But an ordinary man and an ordinary woman and their ordinary children literally alter the destiny of the nations."[5]

Again, that is not to say that politics is irrelevant—far from it. Politics is anything but insignificant. The making and enforcing of laws is a necessary component in ordering a good society (although a society is never orderly or good merely because of the making and enforcing of those laws). Unfortunately, politics is not often viewed as a necessary component in ordering that good society. Instead, politics takes on the illusion of something glamorously enticing and powerful rather than a serviceable function of government. We do our nation a disservice by encouraging the hoopla that surrounds politics.

George Will said it well: "Almost nothing is as important as almost everything in Washington is made to appear. And the importance of a Washington event is apt to be inversely proportional to the attention it receives."[6] Even Eugene McCarthy, once the darling of the New Left, admitted as much, saying, "Being in politics is a lot like being a football coach; you have to be smart enough to understand the game, and dumb enough to think it's important."[7]

Intuitively, citizens acknowledge the empty hype behind politics. According to political analyst E. J. Dionne, that is why most of us are wont to approach politics with more than a little indifference: "Americans view politics with boredom and detachment. For most of us, politics is increasingly abstract, a spectator sport barely worth watching."[8]

Dionne says that since the average person "believes that politics will do little to improve his life or that of his community, he votes defensively," if at all.[9]

As odd as it may seem, that kind of robust detachment from the political processes is actually close to what America's Founding Fathers originally intended. They feared on-going political passions and thus tried to construct a system that minimized the impact of factions, parties, and activists.[10] Citizens were expected to turn out at the polls to vote for men of good character and broad vision—and then pretty much forget about the minute machinations of politics until the next election.[11]

Gouverneur Morris—who actually wrote the first draft of the Constitution and was instrumental in its ultimate acceptance—said, "The Constitution is not an instrument for government to restrain the people, it is an instrument for the people to restrain the government—lest it come to dominate our lives and interests."[12]

The Founding Fathers established a wise system of overlapping checks and balances designed to somewhat de-politicize the arena of statecraft and its attendant statesmanship—as well as to contain politics to the very limited realm of government.

Though there was profound disagreement between Federalists and Anti-Federalists about how much "energy," or "lack thereof," government ought to exercise, there was universal agreement about what John DeWitt called the "peripheral importance of institutional action to the actual liberties of daily life."[13]

Thus, the founders worked together to ensure that the republican confederation of states was as free as possible from ideological or partisan strife.[14] They were not, however, entirely successful, even though much of our history has been marked by the distinct conviction that what goes on next door is of greater immediate concern than what goes on in Washington. But sadly, those days are no more.

Perhaps the most distinctive aspect of our age is the submerging of all other concerns under politics. And thus, we have succumbed to a Lyndon-Johnson-like dependence upon the comprehensive power of the state. The tragic result has been the politicalization of almost all of life.

Faith, Hope, and Politics

And now abide faith, hope, and politics, these three; but the greatest of these is politics. Or so it seems.

In the twentieth century, the smothering influence of ideological politics is evident everywhere. It has wrested control of every academic discipline, of every cultural trend, of every intellectual impulse, even of every religious revival in our time.

Nearly every question, every issue, every social dilemma has been and continues to be translated into legal, judicial, or legislative terms. They are supplied with bureaucratic, mathematical, or administrative solutions. If something is wrong with the economy, then we assume that the government must fix it. If the health care system is inefficient, then we assume that the government must reform it. If education is in disarray, then we assume that the government must revamp it. If family values are absent, then we assume that the government must supply them. And if government itself doesn't work, well then, we naturally assume that the government must reinvent the government. Whatever the problem, it seems that we jump to the conclusion that the government is the sole solution. Salvation by legislation is our credo.

But this modern notion is a far cry from the kind of worldview the American founders and pioneers maintained. They shared a profound distrust of central governments to solve the problems that afflicted individuals, communities, and societies. Certainly, they believed in a strong and active civil authority—but only in its proper place. Thus every brand of statist ideology was abhorred by them.

Thomas Jefferson warned against the danger of "reducing the society to the state or the state to society." Patrick Henry argued, "The contention that the civil government should at its option intrude into and exercise control over the family and the household is a great and pernicious error." Gouverneur Morris insisted that the everyday affairs of society should be designed to avoid what he called the "interference of the state beyond its competence."[15]

Generations later, Senator Henry Cabot Lodge would reiterate their warnings: "Government is but a tool. If ever we come to the place where our tools determine what jobs we can or cannot do, and by what means, then nary a fortnight shall pass in which new freedoms shall be wrested from us straightway. Societal problems are solved by families and communities as they carefully and discriminantly use a variety of tools."[16]

Sadly, such warnings have gone unheeded in our day.

Believing that the dilemmas of the modern age are simply too grave to trust to responsible parents, free markets, vibrant communities, and dynamic private institutions, modern social engineers have erected a sprawling political and ideological kingdom of Babylonian proportions. And still they insist that the "government must do more."[17] Every time a new problem arises, they cry out, "There ought to be a law."

A generation ago Robert Nisbet wrote that the "real significance of the modern state is inseparable from its successive penetrations of man's economic, religious, kinship, and local allegiances, and its revolutionary dislocations of established centers of function and authority."[18]

Similarly the best-selling Canadian author William Gairdner said, "The essence, logic, thrust, and consequence of the modern state—even when this is not the expressed intention—is the invasion and eventual takeover of all private life by the state."[19]

Syndicated columnist Joseph Sobran writes about why this state of government is unhealthy:

The essence of government is force: whatever its end, its means is compulsion. Government forces people to do what they would not otherwise choose to do, or it forces them to refrain from doing what they would otherwise do. So, when we say "government should do x," we are really saying, "people should be forced to do x." It should be obvious that force should be used only for the most serious reasons, such as preventing and punishing violence. The frivolous, improper, or excessive use of force is wrong. We used to call it tyranny. Unfortunately, too many people think that calling for the government to do x is merely a way of saying that x is desirable. And so we are increasingly forced to do things that are not genuine social duties but merely good ideas. The result is that the role of state coercion in our lives grows greater and greater.[20]

A century ago Frederick Bastiat predicted the possibility of a time when politically mesmerized busybodies would "place themselves above mankind." He feared that they would "make a career of organizing it, patronizing it, and ruling it." They would "think only of subjecting mankind to the philanthropic tyranny of their own social inventions." Worst of all, he said, they would "confuse the distinction between government and society."[21]

He was right. That time has come.

❧

Antipolitics

Of course, the danger in underplaying the importance of politics is that our detachment can be transformed into outright apathy.

While E. J. Dionne may have exaggerated the case when he declared that "Americans hate politics," he was not entirely mistaken.[22] According to recent polls, a full 75 percent of the citizenry say that they "have little or

There is no trick to being a humorist when you have the whole government working for you.

—Will Rogers

no confidence in their government." "Our national temper is sour," says Simon Schama, "our attention span limited, our fuse short."[23] We have become more than a little cynical and skeptical.

As H. L. Mencken once said: "The intelligent man, when he pays taxes, certainly does not believe that he is making a prudent and productive investment of his money; on the contrary, he feels that he is being mulcted in an excessive amount for services that, in the main, are useless to him, and that, in substantial part, are downright inimical to him. He sees them as purely predatory and useless."[24]

Mencken further explained the average citizen's suspicion of and distaste for the government, saying, "Men generally believe that they get no more from the vast and costly operations of government than they get from the money they lend to their loutish in-laws."[25]

It is not surprising then that for much of our history, voter registration and turnout have been significantly lower here than in other free societies. Belgium, Australia, Italy, Austria, Sweden, and Iceland all average more than 90 percent participation. Canada, Japan, Britain, Germany, France, Israel, Greece, New Zealand, Luxembourg, Portugal, Spain, Denmark, the Netherlands, and Norway each see over 70 percent of their citizens at the polls. In the United States, however, only slightly more than half of the registered voters ever actually make it to the polls on election day.[26]

Americans have rarely roused themselves sufficiently to get excited about their electoral choices. They generally have found something better to do than vote.

Thus, syndicated columnist Jane Lawrence was hardly exaggerating when she wrote: "Most Americans have yawned their way through what has turned out to be a series of unpleasant exercises in political obfuscation in the last few elections. Perhaps the reason they care more about PTA meetings, zoning hearings, and Rotary luncheons is that in the end, those things actually matter more. It is hard, after all, to get enthusiastic about choices between Tweedle Dee and Tweedle Dum—or to discern what difference such choices might make."[27]

But there is little to justify such tenured ambivalence. The fact is, at a time when government debt, spending, and activist intrusions into our families and communities have grown to almost incomprehensible proportions, our mute citizenship has given the bureaucrats and politicians in Washington tacit approval to lead us ever further down the road to ruin . . . and so, with pied-piper efficiency and aplomb, they have.

During similar times of distress in our nation's history—following the Jeffersonian and Jacksonian eras, immediately after Reconstruction and the Great War, and most recently on the heels of the New Deal and Great Society episodes—Americans have stirred themselves momentarily from their political lethargy to rekindle the fires of freedom. In the face of impending disaster, the collapse of moral resolve, the encroachment of abusive power, and the abnegation of liberty, they committed their lives and their fortunes to the process of political restoration. They proved that one of the great ironies of the American system is that there are times when politics must be treated as a matter of some consequence so that it ceases to be treated as a matter of total consequence.

Clearly, neither politics-as-usual nor the antipolitics of apathy will be sufficient to wrench us out of our nation's cultural malaise. All indications are that our people are ready for change. We want answers. We yearn for a voice of reason. We are tired of the hype, the hyperbole, and the

Of all the tyrannies, a tyranny sincerely expressed for the good of its victims may be the most oppressive. It may be better to live under robber barons than under omnipotent busybodies.

—C. S. Lewis

hypocrisy. We have lost patience with corruption and avarice driving our national agenda while our children are caught in the crossfire of a fierce cultural war. We want action.

Henry Laurens, a member of the Continental Congress and one of the most prominent of the Founding Fathers, challenged his fellow patriots: "At a time when liberty is under attack, decency is under assault, the family is under siege, and life itself is threatened, the good will arise in truth; they will arise in truth with the very essence and substance of their lives; they will arise in truth though they face opposition by fierce subverters; they will arise in truth never shying from the standard of truth, never shirking from the Author of truth."[28]

That is a challenge we would all do well to heed—even today, so far removed from the time when it was first issued. May the good arise.

9

The Fabric of Our Lives

We are perpetually being told that what is wanted is a strong man who will do things. What is really wanted is a strong man who will undo things; and that will be the real test of strength.[1]

—G. K. Chesterton

We all know our society is in trouble. For the most part we can agree on the sundry woes that plague our families, our communities, and our institutional structures. We can quote a litany of statistics documenting rising crime rates, declining educational standards, and the awful prevalence of violence, drugs, sex, corruption, alienation, death, and disaster. And most of us know that the bottom-line issue is a crisis of character.

Where we differ is not so much on the problems but on the solutions. Just look at the divergence of opinions about what we ought to do as a nation in light of the epidemic of juvenile violence. Some have argued that the first task before us in the current climate of violence is to rewrite the juvenile justice code. We argue that we need to be more vigilant in both effectively preventing and properly adjudicating juvenile crime. Unfortunately, though we may all agree that in the days ahead we will have to revisit and revise the way that we currently deal with juvenile offenders, we still can't even pretend to eliminate crime, hostility and hatred, and violent acts among the most vulnerable in our society.

> *We are indeed, the almost chosen people.*
> —Abraham Lincoln

But neither can we erase the very real differences between children and adults—even criminal children and adults. Our system of law recognizes that children are different than adults. We don't let children drive. We don't let them vote. We don't let them smoke. We don't let them drink. We don't let them enter into contracts. We don't let them marry. We don't let them join the military. There are a host of things that we don't allow children to do. We have those laws because we recognize that as children, their frame of reference, their capacity to make decisions, and their ability in judgment is immature.

There might be a temptation to come to a quick solution to the current wave of violence in our culture and simply say, "Let's just treat children as adults." But if we did so, such action would be violating the code of making distinctions between children and adults. A child who commits an adult crime cannot be treated in a childish fashion, but neither can he be treated in the same fashion as an adult criminal.

Some have argued that the culture of violence can only be arrested if we enact stronger, more comprehensive, and more restrictive gun control laws. And while that seems to be a prudent course of action at first glance, it may not be particularly effective. The real argument against severe forms of gun control is not merely one of constitutionality but also of policy, as argued by legal analyst Daniel Polsby: "The conventional wisdom about guns and violence is mistaken. Guns don't increase national rates of crime and violence—but the continued proliferation of gun control laws almost certainly does."[2]

Robert Bork explains: "Gun control laws raise the cost of obtaining a firearm. This is a cost the criminal will willingly pay because a gun is essential to the business he is in. He probably will not have to pay the increased cost because illicit markets adapt to overcome difficulties. There are over 200,000,000 firearms in the United States now, many of them unregistered, and it is easy to smuggle guns in or to make them in basements and garages. A gun need not be state-of-the-art to serve a criminal's purpose. Criminals will never have difficulty getting guns. The citizen who wants a firearm for self-defense will not have access to illicit markets and will be deterred by the higher costs charged in legal transactions. The result is a steady supply of guns for criminal aggression and a diminished supply for self-defense."[3]

Polsby also argues that "it is easy to count the bodies of those who have been killed or wounded with guns, but not easy to count the people who have avoided harm because they had access to weapons. People who are armed make comparatively unattractive victims. A criminal might not know if any one civilian is armed, but if it becomes known that a large number of civilians do carry weapons, criminals will become warier."[4]

While we need to find ways to keep firearms out of the hands of unsupervised youngsters, merely playing fast and free with the Second Amendment is not only likely to be ineffective in stemming the rising tide of violence, it may actually be counterproductive. And so it goes with many of our assumptions about how to cure that which ails our culture.

Heeding Our Heritage

That is why, in the current cultural divide of values, we ought to take a substantial proportion of our cues about the future from the past, learning from the voice of experience. As the literary critic Donald Davidson aptly said: "The past is always a rebuke to the present; it's a better rebuke than any dream of the future. It's a better rebuke because you can see what some of the costs were, what frail virtues were achieved in the past by frail men."[5] In other words, we need to look at what has worked in the past to comprehend what will work in the future. We need to come to terms with our patrimony, our legacy, and our heritage if we are to move ahead with confidence and effectiveness.

The English author and lecturer John H. Y. Briggs has poignantly argued that an historical awareness is essential for the health and well-being of any society, enabling us to know who we are, why we are here, and what we should do: "Just as a loss of memory in an individual is a psychiatric defect calling for medical treatment, so too any community which has no social memory is suffering from an illness."[6]

Lord Acton, the great historian from the previous generation, agreed: "History must be our deliverer not only from the undue influence of other times, but from the undue influence of our own, from the tyranny of the environment and the pressures of the air we breathe."[7]

The venerable aphorism remains as true today as ever: "He who forgets his own history is condemned to repeat it."[8]

It seems that in this awkward new epoch we are afflicted with a malignant contemporaneity. Our preoccupation with ourselves—and thus our ambivalence and ignorance of the past—has trapped us in a recalcitrant present. Renowned historian Daniel Boorstin said:

> In our schools today, the story of our nation has been replaced by social studies—which is the study of what ails us now. In our churches, the effort to see the essential nature of man has been displaced by the social gospel—which is the polemic against the pet vices of today. Our book publishers no longer seek the timeless and the durable, but spend most of their efforts in a fruitless search for . . . la mode social commentary—which they pray will not be out of date when the item goes to press. Our merchandisers frantically devise their new year models, which will cease to be voguish when their sequels appear three months hence. Neither our classroom lessons nor our sermons nor our books nor the things we live with nor the houses we live in are any longer strong ties to our past. We have become a nation of short-term doomsayers. In a word, we have lost our sense of history. Without the materials of historical comparison, we are left with nothing but abstractions.[9]

History is not just the concern of historians and social scientists. It is not the lonely domain of political prognosticators and ivory tower academics. It is the very stuff of life.

Even the most cursory glance at the history of our great land indicates that America was built on at least three essential principles, and upon this triad of values, our culture has been steadfastly secured against the winds of time and circumstance. Faith, family, and work are the simple components of the American spirit—recover them in their fullness and we will recover our cultural equilibrium. These are the cords that weave the gloriously resplendent fabric of our lives. Thus, it would behoove us to look once again upon these great precepts.

When we do this, we find that the American understanding of these ideals is embedded in the Judeo-Christian tradition, which also had a highly significant formative effect on Western civilization in general. So when we consider these three building-block essentials, it is impossible to do so without referencing some of the biblical texts that present and support them. We must also seek to understand these precepts within the framework of the tradition that gave them to us.

❧

Faith

What a person thinks, what he believes, what shapes his ultimate concerns, and what he holds to be true in his heart—in other words, his faith or lack of it—has a direct effect on his material well-being, behavior, and outlook. "For as a man thinks in his heart, so is he" (Prov. 23:7).

In 1905, Max Weber, the renowned political economist and "founding father" of modern sociology, affirmed this fundamental truth for modern social scientists in his classic work *The Protestant Ethic and the Spirit of Capitalism*. He argued that the remarkable prosperity of the West was directly attributable to the cultural, personal, and ethical prevalence of the Judeo-Christian tradition. In contrast to so many other cultures around the globe, where freedoms and opportunities were severely limited and where poverty and suffering abounded, Weber found that faith brought men and nations both liberty and prosperity.

Why does faith have such phenomenal effects?

First, according to our religious heritage, faith reorients all of us fallen and sinful people to reality. Because of our selfish proclivities, we are blind, foolish, ignorant, and self-destructive. More often than not, we are ruled by our passions, lusts, and delusions. We simply have a hard time facing reality without the perspective of faith. Faith in God, however, removes the scales from our eyes and the shackles from our lives (Rom. 5:12–21). In Him, we are at last acquainted with what is right, what is real, and what is true (John 8:32).

Sociologist James Gleason said: "Faith serves us all well as a kind of reality check. It is a transcendent value that enables us to more adequately and objectively evaluate our most bewildering situations and circumstances. In other words, it gives us a perspective beyond our own purblind vantage."[10]

Second, the Judeo-Christian religion also tells us that faith counteracts the destructive effects of sinful actions and activities. Sin is not a concept that has much currency with modern social scientists, economists, politicians, community organizers, civil rights activists, and social service providers. It has become politically incorrect even to speak of sin. Men who have rejected God and do not walk in faith are more often than not immoral, impure, and improvident (Gal. 5:19–21). They are prone to extreme and destructive behavior, indulging in perverse vices and dissipating sensuality (1 Cor. 6:9–10). And they—along with their families and loved ones—are thus driven over the brink of destruction (Prov. 23:21). On the other hand, faith reforms us with new and constructive values (2 Cor. 5:17). We are provoked to moral and upright lives of diligence, purity, sober-mindedness, thrift, trustworthiness, and responsibility (Col. 3:5–15).

According to psychologist Nancy Hellman: "Where poverty, violence, and destruction germinate in the rotting soil of sin, productivity, harmony, and hope flourish in the fertile field of faith. If we were to recover the concept of sin in our society—even from a moderately secularized perspective—we would go a long way toward eradicating the evils of modern life."[11]

Third, faith establishes a future orientation in our hearts and minds. All too often, modern society either flounders in a dismal fatalism or squanders our few resources in irresponsible impulsiveness. Many of us are terribly shortsighted, unmotivated, and naive. And "where there is no vision the people perish" (Prov. 29:18). On the other hand, faith provokes us to live thoughtfully, to plan, to exercise restraint, and to defer gratification in order to achieve higher ends. We are induced to self-control, wisdom, and careful stewardship in order to build for the future.

Bartok Havic, the great Czech historian, supported the idea of faith providing perspective: "History's record is clear: a people who cannot look past the moment, past the fleeting pleasures of fleshly indulgence, will be a people whose culture vanishes from the face of the earth. Ultimately, only faith gives men a sustaining vision for that which is other than their own selfish desires."[12]

Fourth, faith provokes us to exercise responsibility. Outside of the bounds of faith in God, the Bible says we are all naturally prone to selfishness, wastefulness, and sloth (2 Pet. 2:2–3). Faith, on the other hand, enables us to see past ourselves and grow into selfless maturity. We are encouraged to become more responsible in redeeming our time, making the most of every opportunity, and in fulfilling our calling in life. We are bolstered to use our money wisely, to care for our families, to serve the needs of others, and to be an example of redemptive love before all men everywhere. It is this diligent responsibility—the fruit of faith—that we most need if we are ever to recover the American spirit.

"It is faith," says George Gilder, "in all its multifarious forms and luminosities, that can by itself move the mountains of sloth and depression that afflict the world's stagnant economies; it brought immigrants thousands of miles with pennies in their pockets to launch the American empire of commerce; and it performs miracles daily in our present impasse."[13]

Family

The family is the basic building block of society. When the family begins to break down, the rest of society begins to disintegrate. This is particularly evident in the lives of those most vulnerable in our society—women, children, and the poor. A full 75 percent of those living below the poverty line in this country live in broken homes. In times of economic calamity, intact families are ten times more likely to recover and ultimately prosper than broken families.[14]

There is no replacement for the family. The government can't substitute services for it. Social workers can't substitute kindness and understanding for it. Educators can't substitute knowledge, skills, or understanding for it. We all need family to maintain a balanced equilibrium in this hustle-bustle world. We need fathers and mothers and brothers and sisters. We need grandparents, aunts, uncles, and cousins.

"There is no other place," wrote John Chrysostom, "where the human spirit can be so nurtured as to prosper spiritually, intellectually, and temporally, than in the bosom of the family's rightful relation."[15] That is as true today as when he penned those words in the fifth century.

Why is the family so important?

First, family life provides us with a proper sense of identity. In the midst of our families, we can know and be known. We can taste the joys and sorrows of genuine intimacy. We can gain a vision of life that is sober and sure. We are bolstered by the love of family (Luke 11:11–13). We are strengthened by the confidence of family (John 1:39–42). We are emboldened by the legacy of family (Gen. 49:3–27). And we are stabilized by the objectivity of family (Heb. 12:7–11). We all desperately need this kind of perspective. We desperately need to be stabilized in the gentle environs of hearth and home.

Second, family life provides us with a genuine social security. There's no place like home. In times of trouble our greatest resource will always be those who know us best and love us most. Because family members share a common sense of destiny and a bond of intimacy with one another, they can—and will—rush to each other when needed.

"Caesars and Satraps attempt to succor our wounds and wants with opulent circuses and eloquent promises," said Methodius, the famed seventh-century missionary to the Slavs. "All such dolations are mere pretense, however, in comparison to the genuine care afforded at even the coarsest family hearth."[16]

Third, family life provides the accountability and discipline we need. Families are an incubator for sound values (Deut. 6:4–9). They reinforce the principles of authority, structure, liability, obedience, and selflessness. If we do not model accountability and discipline for our children, can we be astounded when they exhibit no trace of upright behavior? How can they learn what is good and noble unless they see it in their families?

According to economist Michael Novak, family accountability and discipline bring out the very best in us: "A typical mother or father, without thinking twice about it, would willingly die, in a fire or accident, say, in order to save one of his or her children. While in most circumstances this human act would be regarded as heroic, for parents it is only ordinary. Thus . . . the Creator has shaped family life to teach as a matter of course the role of virtue."[17]

We need healthy families to pass on the Creator's gifts of virtue, accountability, love, and discipline. We must protect the family to encourage goodness and morality in our culture. Thus, we must aim to strengthen marriages, equip parents, encourage intimacy, and heal brokenness.

> *Americans are, above all, a problem-solving people. They do not believe there is anything in this world that is beyond human capacity to soar and dominate . . . . Full of essential goodwill to each other and to all, confident in their inherent decency and their democratic skills, they will attack again and again the ills in their society, until they are overcome or at least substantially redressed. . . . The great American republican experiment is still . . . the first, best hope for the human race.*
>
> —Paul Johnson

Work

As the Protestant reformer Martin Luther wrote long ago, "the wise, labor with a ready and cheerful heart."[18] Work is the heart and soul, the cornerstone, of the American spirit. Our greatest natural resources include entrepreneurial zeal, private initiative, and personal productivity—not just our rivers, trees, and fertile lands. Our country was founded on a work ethic that motivated and inspired the worker who felt the double blessing of fulfilling his calling and providing for his family in his vocation. Although such sentiment is no longer widely held, it merits re-igniting for numerous reasons:

First, a solid work ethic affords us all a sense of dignity and purpose. It enables us to see ourselves and our daily tasks in terms of a calling (1 Cor. 12:4–6). It enables us to have a sense of satisfaction in having fulfilled another day in performing our God-given task, adding another piece to the puzzle of our destiny. There is real gratification to be had in putting in an honest day's work that cannot be matched by almost any other activity (Exod. 20:9). "A man can do nothing better than to find satisfaction in his work" (Eccles. 2:24), the greatest sage of ancient Israel once said.

Second, a solid work ethic enables us to care for our families, meet our responsibilities, and uphold our values in our communities. We are able to benefit our neighbors, care for the needy, and share with our friends (1 Tim. 5:8). After all, "It is more blessed to give than to receive" (Acts 20:35).

According to sociologist James Gleason: "We must not underestimate the value of a vital work ethic in strengthening the bonds of culture. When individuals are laborious, productive, and diligent, history has shown that community is strong. Where there are incentives for advancement, inducements for enterprise, and opportunities for endeavor, the record of the ages is clear: prosperity will result—regardless of such externals as resources or materials. Diligent work seems to find a way around every obstacle and a solution to every dilemma."[19]

Third, a solid work ethic enables us to leave a legacy for future generations. The emphasis on thrift, diligence, sacrifice, and focus, effectively disciples future generations. They learn from our example, are inspired by our selflessness, and are blessed by our providence. The reason for American prosperity is not accidental. It is the direct outgrowth of the Puritan work ethic, which involved diligent labor, saving, investment, and the philosophy of free enterprise and initiative. We are enjoying the leftover moral capital of those faithful men and women who went before us.

In the words of economist Langdon Lowe: "To lay up a treasury of virtues is as vital a task as laying up a treasury of material goods. Both may be accomplished by our diligence and faithfulness at our daily labors. Both require investment and providence over the long term. Both demand a foresight that is naturally inimicable to the selfish or foolish or impudent or impulsive. But both are the natural domains of the wise."[20]

⁓⨯⁓

A Golden Opportunity

Clearly the task of restoring the fabric of our lives—faith, family, and work—poses problems of giant proportions. It looks like an impossible task. The culture has seemingly gone too far too fast along the downgrade. How can we possibly prevail? I believe we can overcome the same way the biblical David did when he faced a "giant" problem: he stepped out in faith, went to work, and emerged victorious.

To repeat, our best plan of action is (1) to step out in faith, (2) work at this immense task of performing well in our careers and providing support and love for our families, and (3) emerging victorious. We step out in faith, asking God for direction, wisdom, and encouragement, relying on the fact that "All things work together for good to those who love God" (Rom. 8:28). We work at fulfilling our calling, providing a sense of fulfillment and security, while we also work to strengthen and uphold our families. With God's help, we will emerge victorious.

The fact is, freedom-loving people have a golden opportunity to bring about a dramatic reversal in the fortunes of our children and our nation. Nevertheless, to accomplish this great feat we will have to engage ourselves in a struggle against all apparent odds.

Isn't it about time for us to demonstrate to the watching world that Americans can still beat the odds? Isn't it about time for us to prove to a desperately vulnerable generation that they can make a bold stand against all odds and prevail?

Success doesn't happen overnight. Victory doesn't come in a day. A culture is not made or unmade in an instant. So the sooner we get started, the better off we'll be. The sooner we get started, the quicker the victory will come. In order to get from here to there, we need to set out upon the road.

There will never be an ideal time to begin the work of restoring justice and mercy in the land. Money is always short. Manpower is always at a premium. Facilities are always either too small, or too inflexible, or in the wrong location, or too expensive. There is never enough time, energy, or resources.

However, as James Dobson and Gary Bauer have said, "And by all means, let's take heart. America can't be perfect, but it can be better—much better."[21]

So, we should just go forth. Do what we ought to—restoring the fabric of our lives. Starting now.

APPENDIXES

∿∿

A p p e n d i x 1:

C h i l d r e n K i l l i n g

C h i l d r e n

∿∿

Radio Address: March 27, 1998

All of us were shocked and saddened by the tragic shootings Tuesday [March 24] at Westside Middle School near Jonesboro. It's hard to imagine something like that could happen in Arkansas—America's heartland.

I spent the very next day among the victims of this tragedy. I spoke to students, parents, teachers, and others. Everywhere I went, I saw people coming together to share their grief. I met teachers and administrators who had risked their lives to help students caught in the ambush. I saw pastors and counselors offering words of comfort to children and adults. I talked with hospital personnel whose knowledge and skill kept the death toll from rising higher.

In the past few days, my office has received words of support from people across the country and around the world. People may differ on their politics, but everyone can understand the pain involved when a parent loses a child or a child loses a mother.

The four children we lost—Brittney Varner, Paige Herring, Stephanie Johnson, and Natalie Brooks—and the teacher, Shannon Wright, weren't just names and faces in the newspaper. They were part of the Arkansas family. They were five people with hopes and dreams who had so much to look forward to if they had only been given a chance. And the teacher, Shannon Wright, was a hero who jumped between a bullet and the student it was intended for.

At a time like this, all Americans ask one question: Why? It is a question that doesn't have an easy answer. I don't think anyone really understands why bad things happen to good people.

The shootings at Westside are the latest in a series of well-publicized acts of children killing children. It should not surprise us that these things happen in a culture that glorifies violence and devalues life. In our movies, our television, and our music, children are taught for hours each day that violence is easy, pain-less, and without consequence. The lessons learned are that the best ways to solve problems are at the point of a gun.

But it's not honest or fair to lay all of the blame at the feet of the mass media. The images children see on television don't have nearly the impact as the lessons they are taught at home. A child who grows up among violence is more likely to become violent. Violence doesn't always have to be a physical act. In many homes, children live in an atmosphere of distrust and conflict. Often, the only time they are shown attention is when they do something wrong.

In the past few days, many people have offered opinions on how to keep this kind of tragedy from happening again. Some are angry at the law, which does not allow the two suspects to be charged as adults. Many want more security at schools. We're forming a working group to review the state's juvenile justice code, and we'll consider many ideas in the days to come. But we must not act now out of a sense of anger or vengeance. Decisions made in the heat of the moment often aren't the best for the long term.

One thing we must not do is give up on our public schools. You've probably heard someone say in the last couple of days that they weren't going to send their kids to public schools anymore. That's the wrong attitude. Tuesday, 460,000 students across this state went to school in the morning and came home safely that evening, just like every other day. Like every other school in Arkansas, the Westside School District is the center of that community. It gives students a place to learn and adults a place to gather. Thousands of children have learned to read and write there. It has been a place where parents joined with their children to cheer on the Warriors and Lady Warriors. It has been a place where students have dressed up for high school proms, played musical instruments, and performed in plays. It's where lifelong friendships have started and marriages have been born.

Instead of abandoning Westside, the people of that district will draw closer in a spirit of unity and love. The same should happen in the rest of Arkansas. If we want our schools to be safe places of learning, we have to be involved with them. Now is not the time to give up on our schools but to band together to make them stronger.

If we want to live in a peaceful world, we must insist on peaceful homes. We must cultivate a spirit of civility and respect in our families. We must insist that our children solve their differences peacefully, that they seek cooperation, not confrontation. We must never be so busy at work that we don't have time to teach them the values we hold dear. We must be understanding and open, and willing to share the burdens, fears, and frustrations of adolescent life. We must teach our children to do unto others as they would have others do unto them.

We can't change what happened Tuesday at Westside, and we can never bring these five beautiful people back. What we can do is work to make sure they did not die in vain.

The Bible says there's no greater love than when someone lays down his life for friends. Shannon Wright showed that kind of love to the student she saved. Now, it's up to all of us to show that kind of love to the children who remain, at Westside and throughout Arkansas. Let's make sure the two-year-old son Shannon Wright left behind grows up in a world where children feel safe no matter where they are. Let's be ready with a helping hand for those in need, a shoulder to cry on for those in mourning, and ears ready to listen to the questions the children will ask. Let us pray for the injured, the grieving, and, yes, even the accused, knowing full well that God is loving and just. And in honor of the victims of this terrible tragedy, let us move forward to a day when all Arkansas children are given so much love that they never learn to hate.

A p p e n d i x   2:

T h e   J o n e s b o r o   L e g a c y

Radio Address: April 10, 1998

All Arkansans—indeed, all Americans—should be proud of the way the people of Jonesboro and the Westside School District have handled the tragedy that struck their community March 24, 1998. The world has seen their courage and dignity.

There's nothing anyone can say that can take away the pain. Actions, after all, always speak louder than words. That's why it meant so much for the people of Northeast Arkansas to come together, not only for a memorial service broadcast around the world but in the thousands of acts of kindness that have happened every day since the tragedy.

Some members of the media who descended on Jonesboro no doubt wondered if the two boys accused in the shootings represented the people of this state. Some asked if this kind of thing were the direct result of what they called the "Southern culture."

Instead, they got a good taste of what "Southern culture" is really all about, and they shared it with the rest of the world. People everywhere now know the story of Shannon Wright, the teacher who lost her life saving others. They know of Lynette Thetford, another teacher who was shot helping her students. They know of the Reverend Fred Haustein and the other members of the Ministerial Alliance who helped the community heal through the "Service of Hope and Healing." They know of Lisa Lee, who wrote and sang the beautiful song "Heaven's Newest Angel." Most of all, they know of the love and compassion of the people of Arkansas.

Since the shootings, my office has received hundreds if not thousands of phone calls and messages from around the world. Some people are angry that the two boys accused of this terrible crime cannot be charged as adults. I understand their anger, and we fully intend to do something to improve the system. However, we should carefully study all of our options before making changes. Decisions made in the heat of the moment, when passions run high, often result in bad law.

We need to carefully consider our response to this tragedy, study how other states deal with juvenile crime, hear what Arkansans have to say about the issue and then come up with a plan that addresses the problem.

That's why we're forming the Governor's Working Group on Juvenile Justice. The group's coordinator is Kelly Pace, a member of my staff, and it will include people from all walks of life from all parts of Arkansas. Its goal will be not only to find out how we can punish juveniles who commit crimes but also determine how to prevent them from committing crimes in the first place.

One of the most important tasks of the working group will be finding ways to counteract the barrage of violence and conflict children encounter in today's culture. A typical American child will witness 8,000 murders and more than 100,000 acts of violence on television before he graduates from elementary school. One million children each year watch their parents divorce. In Arkansas last year, there were more than 8,500 children abused.

The key to making sure Arkansas' children grow up to be moral, responsible adults is to make sure they have moral, responsible adult role models. Parents must show the kind of love they want their kids to display toward others. Family members and friends must provide positive examples as well as a helping hand to make parenting—the toughest job in the world—a little easier. Others blessed with an abundance of love must be willing to step out of their comfortable social circles to mentor those growing up in broken homes and rough neighborhoods. And society as a whole must realize children are watching and learning.

We'll study if new laws are needed and old laws need changing. But we shouldn't kid ourselves. The best way to change a child's heart isn't by changing the law. The best way to mold a child's character isn't to create more legislation. And the best people to teach children right from wrong aren't politicians in Little Rock or Washington. Parents must love their kids, and society must support parents. Anything else is doomed to failure.

Anytime children kill children, you know there's a problem. However, it's important that we don't let the murderous actions of a few blind us to the goodness of the many. It's true that two young boys are accused of killing four of their classmates and a teacher. But it's also true that half a million students in Arkansas aren't. Despite the violent messages we send them, children across the state are going to school, playing with their friends, and staying out of trouble. They're trying to do right even when some people tell them they would be better off doing wrong.

We shouldn't minimize the tragedy of the shootings at Westside Middle School. Kids who commit crimes should be punished and rehabilitated. But let's not become so focused on a few bad seeds that we ignore the beautiful orchard around us. Most kids are doing fine, and most parents are proud of them.

We should be proud of them too.

A p p e n d i x   3:

C h a r a c t e r   I s

S t i l l   t h e   I s s u e

News Column: January 9, 1998

A doctor who treats the symptoms and not the cause of a disease won't be very successful. The same is true of our society.

No matter what government tries, problems like crime and teen pregnancy persist. That's because these are merely symptoms like the coughing and fever that accompany the flu. In our society, the disease is a lack of character. The virus is the breakdown of the family.

James Q. Wilson, an emeritus professor at the University of California at Los Angeles, said much the same in a recent speech to the American Enterprise Institute. He said we live in two separate nations. In one, children grow up in good homes, get educations, and have successful lives and careers. They enjoy the benefits America offers and expect their futures to be as prosperous as their childhoods have been.

"In the other nation," Wilson said, "a child is raised by an unwed girl, lives in a neighborhood filled with many sexual men but few committed fathers, and finds gang life to be necessary for self-protection and valuable for self-advancement."

Instead of preparing themselves for bright and prosperous futures, he said, those children "live for the moment and think that fate, not plans, will shape their lives."

Wilson said society has done everything it could to solve this problem except the one thing that would actually work: fix the family. "For decades our society has tried to make one nation out of two by changing everything—except the family. We have transferred money from the young to the old to make retirement easier and from rich to poor to make poverty bearable. Congress has devised community action, built public housing, created a Job Corps, distributed food stamps, given federal funds to low-income schools, supported job training, and provided cash grants to working families. States have created new approaches to reducing welfare rolls, and bureaucrats have designed affirmative action programs. We are still two nations."

Wilson said there's a simple explanation: "Governments can transfer money: They cannot build character."

I couldn't agree more. Government can build a school, but teachers won't be able to teach unless children have learned respect for authority at home. Government can put thousands of police officers on the streets, but it can't build prisons fast enough to hold the criminals produced when mothers and fathers don't teach their children right from wrong. Government can raise, train, and equip an army, but there's no defense when a society forsakes the values that hold it together.

Wilson says rebuilding the family won't be easy. He's right. What's needed now isn't so much a new national family policy as a new national commitment to the family, one child at a time.

That will require a change in mind-set. We've grown accustomed to addressing our problems with huge, complicated government programs that, unfortunately, haven't worked and in some cases have made things worse. Instead, we need to ensure government does what it can to help families while avoiding policies that hurt them.

We need a commitment by all parents to strengthening their marriages, households, and communities. That will mean making choices—some of them hard—between what would be easy for the moment and what would be beneficial for a lifetime. It will mean deciding once and for all that our children's futures are more important than our current career paths. And it will mean admitting that the poet John Donne was right, that "no man is an island" and that we have a responsibility to help those families and especially those children who need us. It doesn't take a professor to understand why.

Endnotes

Introduction

1. William Pratt, ed., *The Fugitive Poets* (Nashville: J. S. Sanders, 1991), 130.

2. *U.S. News and World Report,* 6 April 1996.

3. *New York Times,* 2 April 1998.4. *U.S. News and World Report,* 6 April 1998.

5. *Time,* 6 April 1998.

6. *Newsweek,* 6 April 1998.

7. *Covenant Syndicate,* 26 March 1998.

8. *USA Today,* 9 April 1998.

9. *Tennessean,* 16 April 1998.

10. *U.S. News and World Report,* 6 April 1998.

11. James Fenimore Cooper, *The American Democrat* (New York: Knopf, 1931), vii.

Part 1

1. Samuel Johnson, *Omnibus* (London: MacDonald and Stott, 1926), 1: 88.

Chapter 1

1. William Pratt, ed., *The Fugitive Poets: Modern Southern Poetry in Perspective* (Nashville: J. S. Sanders and Company, 1991), 33.

2. Charles Ewing, *Kids Who Kill* (New York: Avon, 1990), 5.

3. William J. Bennett, *The Index of Leading Cultural Indicators* (New York: Simon and Schuster, 1994), 22–23.

4. Ibid., 6–31.

5. U.S. Department of Health, Education, and Welfare, *Violent Schools/Safe Schools: The Safe School Study Report to the Congress,* December 1977.

6. National Center for Education Statistics, *Violence and Discipline Problems in Public Schools: 1996–1997, Executive Summary,* February 1998, 2–4.

7. Ibid.

8. *Washingtonian Magazine,* September 1997.

9. William Bennett, John DiIulio, and John Walters, *Body Count* (New York: Simon and Schuster, 1996).

10. *World,* 11 April 1998.

11. *Booklist,* 15 September 1996.

12. Bennett, *The Index of Leading Cultural Indicators,* 36.

13. *Law Enforcement Review,* May 1997.

14. G. K. Chesterton, *What I Saw In America* (London: Doran, 1935), 14.

15. Alexis de Tocqueville, *Democracy in America* (Boston: Alfred Sloan, 1911), 122.

Chapter 2

1. Samuel Johnson, *An Omnibus of His Wit and Wisdom* (London: Carrel Brothers, 1966), 1:49.

2. *Wall Street Journal,* 24 March 1998.

3. *Forbes,* 14 September 1992.

4. *Life,* February 1941.

5. *Washington Post,* 19 August 1988.

6. *New York Times,* 4 March 1993.

7. *Forbes,* 14 September 1992.

8. *Dimensions,* October 1992, 29.

9. *Forbes,* 14 September 1992.

10. *BBC Report,* 2 November 1980.

11. George F. Will, *Statecraft as Soulcraft* (New York: Simon and Schuster, 1984), 114.

12. *Forbes,* 14 September 1992.

13. Ibid.

14. Ibid.

15. Hilaire Belloc, *Charles the First* (Philadelphia: Lippincott, 1933), 22.

16. William J. Bennett, *The Index of Leading Cultural Indicators* (Washington, D.C.: Empower America/Heritage Foundation/Free Congress Foundation, 1993).

17. George Grant and Mark Horne, *Legislating Immorality* (Chicago: Moody, 1993), 21–47.

18. Jerry Kirk, *The Mind Polluters* (Nashville: Thomas Nelson, 1985), 34–35.

19. Reid Carpenter, *Pittsburgh Leadership Foundation* (Pittsburgh: PLF, 1988), 19.

20. *Report of the Attorney General* (Nashville: Rutledge Hill, 1986).

21. Walter Evans, *The Bordellos of Nevada* (Reno: Desert Visitor, 1979).

22. *Coral Ridge Impact*, May 1990.

23. Cal Thomas, *Things That Matter Most* (Grand Rapids: Zondervan, 1994).

24. William Bennett, *Index of Leading Cultural Indicators* (New York: Simon and Schuster, 1994).

25. Grant and Horne, 109–141.

26. *New York Newsday*, 2 February 1988.

27. Robert H. Bork, *Slouching Towards Gomorrah* (New York: ReganBooks, 1996), 2–3.

28. Ibid., 3.

29. E. Carrington Boggin, *The Rights of Gay People* (New York: Bantam, 1983).

30. *Fort Lauderdale Sun Sentinel*, 14 May 1989.

31. Norman Dorsen, ed., *Our Endangered Rights* (New York: Pantheon, 1984).

32. *Christian Observer*, Spring 1988.

33. Robert Goguet, *The Origin of Laws* (New York: John Taylor, 1821), 302.

34. Ibid., 99.

35. Nathan Villard, *The Founding Era* (New York: Baker, Harbridge, and Wilson, 1958), 47.

36. Gardiner Spring, *The Obligations of the World to the Bible* (New York: Taylor and Dodd, 1821), 101–102.

37. Aleksandr Solzhenitsyn, *A Warning to the West* (New York: Harper and Row, 1978), 64.

38. *Forbes*, 14 September 1992

39. William J. Bennett, *The Index of Leading Cultural Indicators* (Washington, D.C.: Empower America/Heritage Foundation/Free Congress Foundation, 1993).

40. *Houston Chronicle*, 28 March 1998.

41. *USA Today*, 7 April 1998.

42. Stephen Mansfield and Douglas Layton, *Searching for Democracy* (Nashville: Servant Group, 1997), 82.

Part 2

1. Richard Weaver, *Ideas Have Consequences* (Chicago: University of Chicago, 1948), 70–71.

Chapter 3

1. G. K. Chesterton, *A Chesterton Omnibus* (London: Goethe Harramond, 1952), 133.

2. Dave Grossman, *On Killing: The Psychological Cost of Learning to Kill in War and Society* (Boston: Little Brown, 1995), 3–27.

3. Abraham Lincoln, *Letters and Speeches* (Washington, D.C.: Capitol Library, 1951), 341–342.

4. George Grant, *Grand Illusions: The Legacy of Planned Parenthood* (Elkton, Maryland: Highland Books, 1998), 83.

5. George Grant, *Third Time Around: The History of the Pro-Life Movement* (Brentwood, Tennessee: Wolgemuth and Hyatt, 1991), 8–15.

6. George Grant, *Grand Illusions: The Legacy of Planned Parenthood*, 84–104.

7. George Grant, *Killer Angel: The Life of Margaret Sanger* (Windsor, New York: Ars Vitae, 1995), 101–105.

8. George Grant, *Immaculate Deception* (Chicago: Northfield, 1996), 85–104.

9. Grant, *Grand Illusions*, ii, 90.

10. Robert Bork, *Slouching Towards Gomorrah* (New York: ReganBooks, 1996), 179.

11. Grant, *Grand Illusions*, 25.

12. Julia Wittleson, *The Feminization of Poverty* (Boston: Holy Cross Press, 1997), 122–125.

13. Bork, 179.

14. *Family Planning Perspectives*, July/August 1988.

15. Bork, 181.

16. George Grant, *Patriot's Handbook* (Nashville: Cumberland House, 1996), 116.

17. Harold Kane, *Liberty! Cry Liberty!* (Boston: Lamb and Lamb, 1939), 31.

18. Alan Keyes, *Our Character, Our Future* (Grand Rapids: Zondervan, 1996), 6.

Chapter 4

1. *Henry V*, 1.1.54–59.

2. Gary Bauer, *Our Hopes, Our Dreams* (Colorado Springs: Focus on the Family, 1996), 13.

3. Abraham Kuyper, *Observations* (London: English Standard, 1912), 119.

4. John Buchan, *Sundry Occasions* (Toronto: Collins, 1940), 201.

5. Adeline Lang, *The Loss of Civility* (New York: Walter Frasier, 1995), 34–35.

6. Marion Ware, *An Angry Society* (Los Angeles: Veritas Civitas, 1995), xxi–xxii.

7. Ibid., 43.

8. Lang, 34–35.

9. Ibid.

10. David Chagall, *Surviving the Media Jungle* (Nashville: Broadman and Holman, 1996), 21.

11. Ibid.

12. Bryan Griffin, *Panic Among the Philistines* (Chicago: Regnery, 1983), 86, 179.

13. Jonathan Lasker, *Profanity in America* (New York: Colbert Communications, 1996), 17.

14. Ibid.

15. Ibid.

16. Herman Haliburton, *Road Rage* (Dallas: Public Virtues, 1997), 2.

17. *Kansas City MetroScene*, 14 July 1997.

18. Ibid.

19. George Grant, *The Family Under Siege* (Minneapolis: Bethany House, 1994).

20. George Barna, *Absolute Confusion* (Ventura, California: Regal, 1993).

21. James Davison Hunter, *Culture Wars* (New York: Basic Books, 1990), 143–145.

22. Douglas W. Phillips, *The Sinking of the Titanic and Great Sea Disasters* (San Antonio: Vision Forum, 1998), vi.

23. Ibid.

24. *Time*, 30 March 1998.

25. George Washington, *Rules of Civility* (Mt. Vernon, Virginia: Mt. Vernon Association, 1989), 11.

26. Ibid.

Chapter 5

1. Michael Clarke, *Canada: Portraits of Faith* (Chilliwack, British Columbia: Reel to Real, 1998), 109.

2. *Media Analysis*, May 1997.

3. Ibid.

4. Ibid.

5. Clarke, 109.

6. Neil Postman, *Amusing Ourselves to Death* (New York: Penguin, 1985), 155–56.

7. Ibid., vii–viii.

8. Ibid.

9. David Chagall, *Surviving the Media Jungle* (Nashville: Broadman and Holman, 1996), 75.

10. William Bennett, *Index of Leading Cultural Indicators* (New York: Simon and Schuster, 1994), 103.

11. *Media Analysis,* May 1997.

12. Ibid.

13. Bennett, 104.

14. Chagall, 89.

15. *Media Analysis,* May 1997.

16. Bennett, 105.

17. Ibid.

18. Ibid., 106.

19. Chagall, 141.

20. *Media Analysis,* May 1997.

21. Ibid.

22. Bennett, 110.

23. Ibid., 145.

24. Ibid., 142–144.

25. *Media Analysis,* May 1997.

26. Colberg Group, *Anthems of Rage: A Survey of Modern Music Content,* October 1996.

27. Robert Bork, *Slouching Toward Gomorrah* (New York: ReganBooks, 1996), 124.

28. Bennett, 112.

29. Ibid.

30. *Anthems of Rage,* October 1996.

31. Lt. Col. Dave Grossman, *On Killing* (Boston: Little, Brown, 1995), 323.

32. Ibid.

33. Bennett, 113–114.

Chapter 6

1. John Sorelli, *The Family* (Tulsa: King's Signet Books, 1997), 56.

2. *Riverside Bulletin,* July 1992.

3. William Bennett, *Index of Leading Cultural Indicators* (New York: Simon and Schuster, 1994), 8.

4. H. G. Wells, *What Is Coming?* (New York: Macmillan, 1916), 1–2.

5. Paul Johnson, *Intellectuals* (New York: Harper and Row, 1989), 1–2.

6. Ibid.

7. William Gairdner, *The War Against the Family* (Toronto: Stoddart, 1992), 6.

8. Donald Davidson, ed., *I'll Take My Stand* (Baton Rouge: Louisiana State University, 1930), xlvi.

9. Ibid., xxxiii, xl.

10. Sylvia Ann Hewlett, *A Lesser Life* (New York: William Morrow, 1986), 12.

11. Connie Marshner, *Can Motherhood Survive?* (Brentwood, Tennessee: Wolgemuth & Hyatt, 1990).

12. *Atlantic Monthly,* May 1995.

13. Lenore Weitzman, *The Divorce Revolution: The Unexpected Social and Economic Consequences for Women and Children in America* (New York: Free Press, 1985), x.

14. Julia Wittleson, *The Feminization of Poverty* (Boston: Holy Cross, 1983, 1991), 19.

15. Ken Auletta, *The Underclass* (New York: Vintage, 1983), 68.

16. Kim Hopper and Ellen Baxter, *The Private Lives of the Poor* (New York: Community Service Society, 1993), 9.

17. Ibid., 9, 21.

18. Weitzman, x, xii.

19. *USA Today,* 23 June 1991.

20. *Journal of Business Policy Review,* October 1988.

21. *Journal of Business Policy Review,* May 1991.

22. *USA Today,* 11 February 1992.

23. Hewlett, 71.

24. Ibid., 72.

25. *Journal of Business Policy Review,* October 1988.

26. Thomas Sowell, *Civil Rights* (New York: William Morrow, 1984), 100.

27. Peyton Moore, *Tales from the Front* (London: L.L. Johnson and Sons, 1902), 215.

28. *New York Times,* 12 June 1988.

29. Madeline Gray, *Margaret Sanger* (New York: Richard Marek, 1979), 203–244.

30. *USA Today,* 3 April 1993.

31. Auletta, 68.

32. Ibid., 69.

33. *USA Today*, 3 April 1993.

34. Robert Ruff, *Aborting Planned Parenthood* (Houston: New Vision, 1988), 89.

35. David Chilton, *Power in the Blood* (Brentwood, Tennessee: Wolgemuth & Hyatt, 1987), 51.

36. *Family Planning Perspectives*, October 1986.

37. *National Right to Life News*, 15 April 1995.

38. Ruff, 89.

39. John T. Wilson, *Abortion and Repentance* (Los Angeles: Life Light Press, 1988).

40. Randy Alcorn, *Pro-Life Answers to Pro-Choice Arguments* (Portland: Multnomah, 1992), 137–164.

41. *The New American*, 20 January 1986.

42. William Sloan, *Safe and Legal? Medical Risks and Hazards* (London: Pro Vitas Europe, 1994), 112.

43. Ibid.

44. Wittleson, 81.

45. *Riverside Bulletin*, July 1992.

46. Mary Pride, *The Way Home: Beyond Feminism, Back to Reality* (Wheaton, Illinois: Crossway Books, 1985), 224.

47. Robert Bork, *Slouching Towards Gomorrah* (New York: ReganBooks, 1994), 154.

48. *Public Agenda*, December 1995.

49. Bork, 157.

50. Ibid.

51. Bennett, 45.

Chapter 7

1. James Tolbert, *The Poetic Genius* (London: Faber and Faber, 1966), 43.

2. *People*, 13 April 1998.

3. Ibid.

4. Ibid.

5. William Bennett, *The De-Valuing of America* (New York: Summit, 1992), 42.

6. Thomas Sowell, *Inside American Education: The Decline, the Deception, the Dogmas* (New York: Free Press, 1993).

7. Bennett, 42–44.

8. *Education Reporter*, November 1993.

9. *Forbes*, 7 June 1993.

10. Dan Alexander, *Who's Running Our Schools: The Case Against the NEA Teacher Union* (Washington, D.C.: Save Our Schools, 1988), 6–7.

11. Ibid.

12. Phoebe Courtney, *Target: America's Children* (Littleton, Colorado: Independent American, 1989), 15.

13. Ibid.

14. *The National Education Review,* March 1998.

15. Ibid., 16.

16. Sally Reed, *NEA: Propaganda Front of the Radical Left* (Alexandria, Virginia: National Council for Better Education, 1984), 32–33.

17. *Forbes,* 7 June 1993.

18. Courtney, 14.

19. Francis DelVoe, *Education in Crisis* (Denver: Littlefield, 1990), 200.

20. *Tennessean,* 18 November 1993.

21. Charles Barrett, *The National Education Association* (Portland: Public School Renewal Association, 1997), 88.

22. *Forbes,* 7 June 1993.

23. Alexander, 89.

24. *Forbes,* 7 June 1993.

25. Barrett, 82–88

26. Ibid.

27. Courtney, 51.

28. Barrett, 89.

29. Samuel Blumenfeld, *NEA: Trojan Horse in American Education* (Boise: Paradigm, 1984), x.

30. Ibid.

31. Alexander, 101.

32. Reed, 41.

33. Alexander, 85.

34. Ibid.

35. *Forbes,* 7 June 1993.

36. Alexander, 88.

37. Barrett, 84.

38. Ibid.

39. Alexander, 109.

40. Barrett, 93.

41. Ibid., 80–88.

42. Ibid.

43. Alexander, 127.

44. Barrett, 76.

45. Alexander, 134.

46. *Phyllis Schlafly Report,* September 1993.

47. Courtney, 16–17.

48. *Phyllis Schlafly Report,* September 1993.

49. Barrett, 93.

50. *New Republic,* 18 April 1981.

51. Barrett, 93.

52. *Phyllis Schlafly Report,* May 1993.

53. Ibid.

54. Barrett, 82.

55. *Empowerment,* March 1993.

56. *Advocate,* 15 December 1992.

57. Ibid.

58. James Bennett and Thomas DiLorenzo, *Official Lies* (Alexandria, Virginia: Groom, 1992), 190.

59. Charles Leslie Glenn, *The Myth of the Common School* (Amherst, Massachusetts: University of Massachusetts, 1988), 143.

60. Barrett, 77.

61. Ibid.

62. Glenn, 143.

63. Barrett, 41.

64. *Learning for a Lifetime,* June 1989.

65. Ibid.

66. John Henry Newman, *The Idea of a University* (Chicago: Loyola University, 1927), v.

67. Ibid., vi.

68. Ibid.

69. Susan Schaeffer Macaulay, *For the Children's Sake* (Westchester, Illinois: Crossway, 1984), 2.

70. James Q. Wilson, *The Moral Sense* (New York: Basic Books, 1992).

71. G. K. Chesterton, *Stories, Poems, and Essays* (London: J. M. Dent, 1951), 84.

Part 3

1. Calvin Coolidge, *Autobiography* (Boston: Leverett Brothers, 1929), 223.

Chapter 8

1. Barton Leland Moore, *James A. Garfield: A Memorial* (New York: Holmberg Brothers, 1881), 271.

2. Elizabeth Frost-Knappman, ed., *The World Almanac of Presidential Quotations* (New York: Pharos, 1993), 165.

3. Evetts Haley, *A Texan Looks at Lyndon: A Study in Illegitimate Power* (Canyon, Texas: Palo Duro, 1964).

4. *Nashville Banner,* 25 January 1993.

5. G. K. Chesterton, *The Common Man* (London: Sheed and Ward, 1932), 34.

6. *Washington Post,* 5 July 1990.

7. Jon Winokur, *The Portable Curmudgeon* (New York: Penguin, 1987), 220.

8. F. J. Dionne, *Why Americans Hate Politics* (New York: Simon and Schuster, 1991), 9.

9. Ibid., 18.

10. *Remnant Review,* 6 November 1992.

11. James Reichley, *The Life of the Parties* (New York: Free Press, 1992), 22.

12. Michael Drummond, *Participatory Democracy in the Making* (New York: Carnell, 1923), 19.

13. Ibid., 17.

14. Ross Lence, *Union and Liberty* (Indianapolis: Liberty, 1992).

15. Horton Kael and William Loomis, *A Documentary History of Liberal Thought* (New York: Cushman, 1959), 163, 228.

16. Ibid., 331.

17. *State of the Union Address,* 17 February 1993.

18. William D. Gairdner, *The War Against the Family* (Toronto: Stoddart, 1992), 6.

19. Ibid.

20. *Senior American,* December 1993.

21. Frederick Bastiat, *The Rule of Law* (Irvington-on-Hudson, New York: Foundation for Economic Education, 1950).

22. Dionne, 9-11.

23. *Forbes,* 14 September 1992.

24. H. L. Mencken, *A Mencken Chrestomathy* (New York: Vintage, 1982), 8.

25. H. L. Mencken, *Quotations from a Curmudgeon* (New York: Legget, 1967), 41.

26. Frances Fox Piven and Richard A. Cloward, *Why Americans Don't Vote* (New York: Pantheon, 1988), 5.

27. *Augusta Picayune,* 5 November 1992.

28. Henry L. Bell, *Under the Articles* (New York: Scribners, 1921), 122.

Chapter 9

1. G. K. Chesterton, *What I Saw In America* (New York: Dodd Mead, 1922), 128.

2. *American Enterprise,* May 1995.

3. Robert Bork, *Slouching Towards Gomorrah* (New York: ReganBooks, 1996), 167.

4. *American Enterprise,* May 1995.

5. Donald Davidson, ed., *I'll Take My Stand* (Baton Rouge: Louisiana State University, 1930), xxx–xxxi.

6. Tim Dowley, ed., *Handbook to the History of Christianity* (Grand Rapids: Eerdmans, 1977), 2.

7. Ibid.

8. Michael Laughton-Douglas, *Truer Truth Than This* (London: Haverford, 1978), 84.

9. *Newsweek,* 6 July 1970.

10. James Gleason, *The Social Dynamic of Faith* (New York: Harbor Lane Books, 1956), 203.

11. Nancy Hellman, *The Concept of Sin* (Chicago: Watertower Books, 1966), xxi.

12. Kyle Peters, *Voices from the East* (Paris: YMCA Press, 1956), 302.

13. George Gilder, *Wealth and Poverty* (New York: Basic Books, 1981), 75.

14. James Easton, *Poverty and the Family* (New York: Social Service Society, 1991), 132.

15. Michael Fulbright, *Disciples of the Patristics* (Cresswell, New York: Monastery Press, 1988), 97.

16. Fulbright, 58.

17. Michael Novak, *The Spirit of Democratic Capitalism* (New York: Simon and Schuster, 1982), 122.

18. Fulbright, 209.

19. Gleason, 184.

20. Fulbright, 165.

21. *USA Today,* 7 April 1998.

BECAUSE CHARACTER
Does Matter

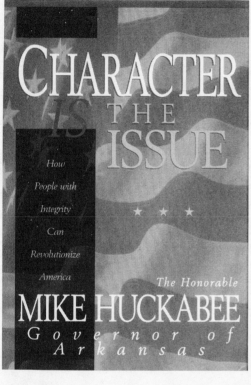

On July 15, 1996, Mike Huckabee, a former Baptist pastor, was preparing for his swearing-in ceremony as governor of Arkansas. He was supposed to replace Jim Guy Tucker, who was resigning in the wake of mail fraud and conspiracy convictions in the Whitewater scandal. At the last minute, however, Tucker refused to relinquish control. Here for the first time anywhere is Governor Huckabee's own complete account of that incredible day and the events leading up to it. Huckabee also discusses his years in ministry and presents his vision for a government grounded in Christian character and solid moral values.

Character IS the Issue (hardcover)   0-8054-6367-4

Available at fine bookstores everywhere